P9-CPZ-677

PHILOSOPHY OF RELIGION SERIES

General Editor's Note

The philosophy of religion is one of several very active branches of philosophy today, and the present series is designed both to consolidate the gains of the past and to direct attention upon the problems of the future. Between them these volumes will cover every aspect of the subject, introducing it to the reader in the state in which it is today, including its open ends and growing points. Thus the series is designed to be used as a comprehensive textbook for students. But it is also offered as a contribution to present-day discussion; and each author will accordingly go beyond the scope of an introduction to formulate his own position in the light of contemporary debates.

JOHN HICK

Philosophy of Religion Series

General Editor: John Hick, H. G. Wood Professor of Theology,
University of Birmingham

Published

John Hick (Birmingham University) Arguments
for the Existence of God
H. P. Owen (King's College, London) Concepts of Deity
Kai Nielsen (Calgary University)
Contemporary Critiques of Religion
Terence Penelhum (Calgary University)
Problems of Religious Knowledge
M. J. Charlesworth (Melbourne University)
Philosophy of Religion: The Historic Approaches
William A. Christian (Yale University) Oppositions of Religious Doctrines:
A Study in the Logic of Dialogue among Religions
Ninian Smart (Lancaster University) The Phenomenon of Religion
Hywel D. Lewis (King's College, London) The Self and Immortality
Basil Mitchell (Oriel College, Oxford)
The Justification of Religious Belief

Forthcoming titles

Nelson Pike (California University)
Religious Experience and Mysticism
Donald Evans (Toronto University) Religion and Morality
Dennis Nineham (Keble College, Oxford) Faith and History
George Mavrodes (University of Michigan)
God and the World
Ramchandra Gandhi (Delhi University)
Humanism

THE JUSTIFICATION
OF RELIGIOUS BELIEF

BASIL MITCHELL

Nolloth Professor of the Philosophy
of the Christian Religion, University of Oxford,
and Fellow of Oriel College

A Crossroad Book
THE SEABURY PRESS · NEW YORK

© Basil Mitchell 1973

First published 1973 by
THE MACMILLAN PRESS LTD
London and Basingstoke
Associated companies in New York
Dublin Melbourne Johannesburg and Madras
and
THE SEABURY PRESS
815 Second Avenue
New York, N.Y. 10017

Library of Congress Cataloging in Publication Data

Mitchell, Basil.
  The justification of religious belief.

  (Philosophy of religion series)
  "A Crossroad book."
  1. Religion—Philosophy. I. Title.
BL51.M654   200'.1   73-17904
ISBN 0-8164-1152-2

Contents

Preface   vii

Acknowledgements   viii

Introduction   1

PART I

1 CAN GOD'S EXISTENCE BE DISPROVED?   7

2 CAN GOD'S EXISTENCE BE PROVED?   21

PART II

3 THE NATURE OF A CUMULATIVE CASE   39

4 A STRATEGY FOR THE DEFENCE OF THE RATIONALITY OF THEISM   59

5 RATIONAL CHOICE BETWEEN SCIENTIFIC PARADIGMS   75

PART III

6 FAITH AND KNOWLEDGE   99

7 RATIONALITY AND COMMITMENT   117

8 FAITH AND REVELATION   135

Notes   157

Select Bibliography   170

Index   177

Preface

This book was originally to have been entitled 'The Language of Religion' but at an early stage, like some characters in fiction, it took on a life of its own, and assumed a different subject which in turn dictated a different title. I am indebted to Professor John Hick, as editor of the series, for his toleration of this change and his help throughout.

Mr J. R. Lucas and Mr M. R. McLean kindly read the greater part of the manuscript and helped me with suggestions and criticisms, and I owe a debt of gratitude to them and to the many graduate students in the philosophy of religion at Oxford who have discussed the problems involved at various stages. One is never more acutely aware of the inadequacies of a work than at the time of writing the preface, nor of one's own responsibility for them.

Lastly I should like to thank Mr R. F. D. Collin, who prepared the manuscript for publication in an exemplary manner, and Mr P. A. Byrne, who helped with the bibliography.

BASIL MITCHELL

Oriel College, Oxford
January 1973

Acknowledgements

The author and publishers are grateful for permission for quotations from the following: Cleanth Brooks and Douglas Bush, 'Marvell's Horatian Ode', from *The Sewanee Review*, Vol. 60 # 3, summer 1952, reprinted by permission; I. M. Crombie, 'Theology and Falsification', from *New Essays in Philosophical Theology*, ed. Antony Flew and A. MacIntyre, by permission of SCM Press Ltd and Macmillan Publishing Co Inc., New York; D. D. Evans, 'Differences between Scientific and Religious Assertion', from *Science and Religion: New Perspectives on the Dialogue* by permission of SCM Press Ltd. and Harper and Row Inc.; Antony Flew, *God and Philosophy*, by permission of Hutchinson Publishing Group Ltd and Harcourt Brace Jovanovich Inc.; T. S. Kuhn, *The Structure of Scientific Revolution* by permission of the University of Chicago Press; A. Musgrave and I. Lakatos, *Criticism and the Growth of Knowledge*, by permission of Cambridge University Press; J. A. Passmore, 'The Objectivity of History', from *Philosophy*, Vol. 33, 125 (1958), by permission of the Royal Institute of Philosophy; W. H. Walsh, *Metaphysics*, by permission of Hutchinson University Library; John Wisdom, 'Gods', from *Proceedings of the Aristotelian Society*, Vol. XIV (1944/45) © The Aristotelian Society, 1945, pp. 185–206.

Introduction

The question I want to discuss is whether religious belief requires or admits of rational support; if so, of what sort and to what extent. It is an old problem and the absence of an agreed solution may suggest that it is unprofitable to pursue it further. However, the list of agreed answers to philosophical questions is short and the adoption of this policy would put an end to most philosophical inquiry. We should not expect to reach agreement on fundamental issues easily.

Nevertheless to discover the role of reason in matters of religion does appear to be peculiarly difficult. A man's position is comparatively rarely affected by explicit argument and the more profoundly religious, or indeed anti-religious, he is the less likely is he to be argued out of it. It is, in religious terms, a matter of faith. One consequence of this is that the word 'theology' and its cognates is increasingly used of any body of convictions which is not readily subjected to criticism, usually with the implication that they have little immediate practical relevance. It is in this transferred sense that a political commentator will describe a debate at the Labour Party Conference as a 'theological' one.

The possibility of this usage indicates, however, that there is at the very least some analogy between religion and politics in this respect. In politics, as in religion, men become committed to positions which they will not readily give up and which involve their entire personalities. On neither of these subjects are differences easily resolved by argument; hence the convention that they are unsuitable subjects for ordinary polite conversation. Moreover, when argument does take place (for example, on television), it is often felt to be superficial and even slightly absurd. Much discussion about religion, like much political discussion, strikes the uncommitted, and even the seriously committed, as little more than

1

undignified posturing, in which the opponents go through the motions of rational debate without the serious expectation of persuading or being persuaded.

In spite of this, however, where political convictions are at issue there are few who would willingly concede that no question of justification arises. It is not so much that argument is entirely inappropriate as that it is likely in practice to be ineffective. Where fundamental beliefs are under attack, as when liberal democracy is exposed to a Marxist critique, the individual tends to feel both that the critic's case has force and that he is ill-equipped to meet it. He cannot dismiss it as irrelevant nor can he readily identify and refute its errors. The situation is one in which rational argument, if it is possible at all, is bound to be complex and difficult and in which there is a disinclination to be entirely swayed by it. A satisfactory account of the sort of reasoning involved should render this situation intelligible.

There are, no doubt, important differences between religion and politics which affect the character of fundamental debate about them. There are reasons why such debate is even more difficult in religion than in politics, and due attention must be paid to them. But it is important first to notice the similarities in the problems they raise. Religion is too often discussed as if the intellectual difficulties associated with it were entirely peculiar to it; as if, outside the religious sphere, men were faced only with problems to which clear and straightforward solutions could in principle be found, however intractable they might prove in practice. The programme of logical positivism gained much of its appeal from the proposal to mark a sharp distinction between the realm of science and common sense on the one hand and the region of theology and metaphysics on the other, and the temptation still persists. In what follows I have deliberately moved from non-theological to theological examples in the hope that only those features of the theological case will be taken as peculiar to it which really are so.

My intention, then, is to give an account of the sort of reasoning by which a religious position is characteristically supported which will do justice to the way in which debate

2

about religious questions actually proceeds and to the role which reason plays in the believer's life. I shall claim that there are important resemblances in this respect between religious and other fundamental convictions. Although my concern is, thus, entirely general I propose to take as an example a particular system of religious belief, what I shall call 'traditional Christian theism' [1]. I use the term 'traditional' rather than 'orthodox' because I do not wish to imply that it represents what the contemporary Christian ought to believe and thus beg the question against those modern theologians who would depart more or less radically from the traditional scheme. It has to be a particular system of religious belief because there is no such thing as 'religion as such'. The attempt to define 'religion' is a notoriously difficult exercise and one which would, in any case, be unprofitable for my purpose, since 'religion' so defined would not be what anyone seriously believed in or was seriously concerned to defend or attack. Traditional Christian theism has a long and distinguished intellectual history; it has been subjected to closer critical analysis and been more carefully elucidated than any other system of religious belief and it is still what the ordinary educated man understands by Christianity, what he accepts if he calls himself a Christian or rejects if he calls himself an atheist.

It would be a mistake to insist on too precise a formulation of this traditional Christian theism. It is, of course, open to various interpretations. All that is necessary is that the range of interpretations permitted should not be so wide as to prevent its being used effectively as an example. Thus it seems reasonable to regard deism – the belief that God has created the world but does not intervene in it – as an alternative to Christian theism rather than a variant of it, whereas the question whether God's eternity implies that he is timeless can be taken to arise with Christian theism itself. Similarly a limited God, such as is proposed by some 'process theologians', may reasonably be taken as an alternative to God as traditionally conceived, but the question whether God is capable of suffering can be raised within the traditional scheme. These decisions are not arbitrary; they

3

reflect the conviction that certain features of the traditional system are more fundamental than others and affect more radically the sort of case that can be made for it. By allowing some degree, but not too great a degree, of flexibility I hope to be able to discuss a version of Christianity that is not too narrowly defined, but has, nevertheless, a recognisable structure.

The book falls into three parts. The first of these is concerned with the question whether traditional Christian theism can be proved or disproved. The argument of this part is necessarily condensed, but I felt bound to give some indication of my reasons for assuming in the remainder of the book that neither is possible. In the course of the discussion certain themes emerge which are relevant to the main argument, but many readers may prefer to start at Part II. In this I introduce and illustrate the conception of a cumulative argument and contend that metaphysical and theological positions are characteristically supported by such arguments. In Part III I examine the implications of this analysis for the problem of the nature of faith and the relation between faith and reason, and suggest that there are important resemblances between religious and non-religious cases.

Part I

1 Can God's Existence be Disproved?

In recent years philosophical criticism of theism has tended to take the form of an attempt to show that it is logically inconsistent, or in some other way logically incoherent through failing some legitimate test of significance or intelligibility. If that could be shown there would be no room for an examination of the rational case for theism of the sort I want to undertake. Not only could there be no good reason for belief in God; there would be no possibility of its being even a matter of faith. The subject has accumulated a considerable literature [1], and the present treatment will inevitably be summary and selective. But it would be wrong to evade the challenge altogether and, in meeting it, we are likely to encounter considerations which will be of importance in the later argument.

The charge most commonly made, to which Kai Nielsen in his recent book gives a great deal of attention [2], is that it is inconsistent to assert both that God is incorporeal and that he loves or judges or forgives or is the subject of any other psychological predicates. For such predicates can only be ascribed to a being who is capable of action, and action is not possible without a body. In other words divine agency has to be understood on the analogy of human agency; and all human agency can be traced back to the agent's body.

The theist is bound to agree that he does rely on this analogy. The question is whether our concept of action is such as to render unintelligible all talk of incorporeal agency. It is worth noting, to begin with, that the language in which we describe actions is logically distinct from that in which we describe physical movements. It presupposes a conscious agent with intentions and purposes which he attempts to

7

realise in his environment as he sees it. Actions may be done through the agency of others, and events which are not physical, such as concentrating and deciding, may be regarded as actions. Moreover there has been a good deal of research into telekinesis, the alleged power to alter events such as the fall of dice by simply 'willing'. Whether or not telekinesis actually occurs, it does not seem difficult to specify the conditions under which we should be prepared to admit its occurrence. If the dice were to fall with a certain number upwards whenever a particular individual was asked to bring it about and not otherwise, we should conclude that he had the power to cause physical changes without bodily movement [3]. Bodily movement on the part of the agent is normally a reliable guide as to whether an occurrence is an action or not, and, if so, whose; but we could, in principle, settle both questions without recourse to this criterion, if the other indications were clear enough. What are these? A combination of the following:

(i) The unlikelihood of the event's occurrence apart from the intervention of some agent.

(ii) The event's contributing to some purpose.

(iii) The agreement of that purpose with the independently known character and purposes of the putative agent.

Whether there are any events that have actually occurred which satisfy these requirements enough to justify our regarding them as due to divine agency and whether, in any case, we can have any independent knowledge of the character and purposes of God are questions about which theists and atheists are in dispute. The present point is, simply, that the possibility cannot be ruled a priori on the sole ground that incorporeal agency is unintelligible.

Another attempt to show that the concept of God is inconsistent is by way of what is sometimes called 'the ontological disproof of the existence of God'. It is associated particularly with the name of J. N. Findlay [4] and runs as follows. God is thought of traditionally as a being whose existence is, in some sense, necessary. It cannot be the case with respect to God that he just happens to exist. Such a God would not be a suitable object of worship. But to say that

8

God necessarily exists is to say that it is logically impossible that he should not exist; and this notion of a being whose existence is logically necessary is itself logically impossible. There is, therefore, no such being as God is represented to be.

A different route to the same conclusion is by way of the demand for explanation. If we look for an answer to the question 'Why does anything at all exist?', the only possible explanation would have to lie in the existence of a being about whose existence the same question could not be asked; that is to say, a being which is self-explanatory, which cannot be conceived not to exist. And it is just such a 'necessary being' that is logically objectionable [5].

As will emerge in our treatment of the ontological argument in the next chapter [6], the conclusion is to be accepted that God cannot be thought of as a 'necessary being' if by that is meant a being whose existence is logically necessary. But this involves a refutation of theism only if theists are committed to this conception of God; and in fact they are not. What is essential to the traditional idea of God is that he should be thought of as depending on nothing else for his existence, for only so can he be worshipped as Creator of the universe. But there need be no contradiction involved in the denial that there is a being who depends on nothing else for his existence. Whether there is such a being is a question which cannot be settled by logic alone.

The inconsistencies in theism which we have been considering, if they are inconsistencies at all, are not readily apparent. It requires a certain degree of philosophical sophistication to suspect their existence. But there is one problem about the consistency of theism which manifestly arises and which is rightly thought to be crucial for religious faith – the problem of evil.

The alleged inconsistency in this case is between three propositions to each of which Christians are committed:
(i) God exists and is omnipotent and omniscient.
(ii) God is perfectly good.
(iii) The world contains instances of evil.

The inconsistency arises, it is claimed, because a being who was perfectly good would prevent evil if it was in his power to do so. It is this assumption which the theist is bound to contest, since it overlooks the possibility that there might be morally sufficient reasons for God's permitting evil. It is not simply evil, but pointless and irredeemable evil, which would be incompatible with the character of God as Christians conceive him. Hence the critic who claims to demonstrate an inconsistency in theism has to show that there could be no way of justifying the evil in the world.

It is important to notice that in this dispute the onus of proof is upon the critic of theism; for he has undertaken the stringent task of demonstrating an inconsistency in the theist's case. It is, therefore, not enough for him to cast some doubt on the ways in which theists have sought to deal with this problem; he has to show that it is logically impossible that God should have a morally sufficient reason to allow evil of the sort that we encounter in the world [7]. According to traditional Christian belief the purpose of God's creation is that men should finally enjoy a communion with one another and with God which fully satisfies their hearts and minds, and the present world, with its suffering and its opportunities for moral evil, provides the only sort of environment in which men could develop the virtues needed to sustain and enjoy that status. Believing this and believing also, as Christians, that God has involved himself in the suffering of the world and, in so doing, shown how it may be transmuted, believers claim that they have been given some insight, however incomplete, into the mystery of evil.

This entire theistic scheme has been the subject of intense philosophical controversy, turning on such questions as the compatibility of divine omnipotence and human freedom, the possibility of an after life, whether men could have been created wholly good; and these questions and others like them [8] are clearly at issue in the debate between theism and atheism. The positions taken by the disputants appear to reflect, as might be expected, conflicting metaphysical positions, and there is little reason for believing that the philosophical critics of theism have succeeded in showing, in a manner independent of such metaphysical controversy, that the theistic scheme is inconsistent.

Strict logical inconsistency is only one of the ways in
10

which a system of belief might fail of intelligibility, and ever since the publication in 1936 of A. J. Ayer's 'Language, Truth and Logic', the philosophical critique of religion has tended to concentrate upon two important respects in which theism is held to be logically incoherent. The first is that theistic statements are unverifiable; the second that, in the case of statements about God, there is no way of telling what one is talking about.

These criticisms have recently been restated with considerable force by Nielsen [9]. His claim is that any statement which purports to be a statement of fact must satisfy the following requirement: 'Some experiential events, processes or states, if they were to occur or to obtain, must count for or against the truth of a factual statement' [10]. He complains that much of the criticism of the verifiability criterion has been directed against a restricted version of it: that which demands *conclusive* verification or falsification. One criticism, however, which has been directed against the more liberal version is that it is so wide as to allow theological and metaphysical statements to qualify as factual, and it is this criticism which Nielsen is especially concerned to rebut. It is my view that he fails to rebut it, and that theistic statements can indeed satisfy this version, which is by far the most plausible version, of the verifiability criterion. Whether even this version of the verifiability principle is in fact tenable I am content to leave undecided [11]. The reason for Nielsen's failure, as I see it, is that he does not consistently adhere to the version of the verifiability criterion which he has chosen to adopt, but regresses at crucial points in his argument to a more stringent version, which he has earlier repudiated. This emerges most clearly in his discussion of John Hick's concept of 'eschatological verification' [12]. Hick claims that, in the case of theism, there is an asymmetry between verification and falsification. An assertion like 'God governs the world' cannot be conclusively falsified, but it could, in principle, be conclusively verified in a life beyond death. We can conceive, that is to say, a

situation which points unambiguously to the existence of a living God, *viz.* (a) an experience of the fulfillment of

11

God's purpose for ourselves, as this has been disclosed in the Christian revelation and (b) an experience of communion with God as he has revealed himself in the person of Christ [13].

Nielsen's objection to this is that Hick has not succeeded in meeting the stated requirement; for the experiences in question are all described in theistic terms ('the fulfillment of God's purpose', 'communion with God', 'the person of Christ') and it is precisely this sort of language whose intelligibility is in dispute. Hick has failed to describe, in terms which are intelligible to theist and atheist alike, the experiences which would remove all rational doubt about theism. This criticism is, as it stands, justified; but it is only decisive if Hick could not do what Nielsen asks him to do, describe in non-theistic terms the situation which he has been describing in theistic terms. Let us now attempt this.

Suppose that the individual is aware of having survived death and finds himself in a situation which, if not literally identical with traditional representations of the blessed in heaven, is such that he can recognise it as what they were attempting to represent. He is in the company of men who display all the signs of intense happiness and deep mutual affection. They are in the presence of a figure who is recognisable as Jesus and they accept his authority without constraint. In him they experience an overwhelming sense of majesty and holiness of character that calls to mind, only now with far greater intensity, their moments of devotion on earth. Jesus (as on the journey to Emmaus) discloses to each of them the true meaning, as he is now able to judge, of his entire spiritual history, making clear to him how the ills he had suffered had contributed to an intelligible pattern which is now recognisably complete. Would not these experiences, taken together with others of a similar kind, which we need not specify, suffice to put the truth of traditional Christian theism beyond reasonable doubt?

Nielsen does not address himself directly to this possibility, but he says enough in passing to indicate what his response would be. He would argue that to take the

12

experiences, described in this way, as confirming theism would involve interpreting them theistically and that it is open to a sceptic to interpret them otherwise. He says [14]:

> We have no idea at all what must be the case for it to be true or even probably true, or false or even probably false, that our lives have a final destiny or purpose. And we do not know, not even vaguely, what needs to happen for us to be able to assert correctly that a certain state of affairs is apprehended as the fulfillment of God's purpose *and not simply as a natural state of affairs*.. [my italics]

Here Nielsen seems to be rejecting, somewhat dogmatically, precisely the sort of empirical evidence that he has been demanding all along – for no other reason than that other interpretations of it are logically possible. This is immediately confirmed by what follows [15]:

> There are no experiences, actual or conceivable, post-mortem or otherwise, which would even infirm the sceptic's putative assertion and confirm the theist's. They are both equally compatible with anything and everything that could be experientially specified. Or to put it more modestly and in the form of a challenge, what is the *factual* and not *purely verbal* difference between these two claims?

What Hick is claiming, as I am now· interpreting his position, is that it is possible to specify a state of affairs, described in accordance with Nielsen's requirements in non-theistic terms, which is such that, if it occurred, a theistic interpretation of it would be far more convincing that any other. *A fortiori*, that state of affairs is one which tends to give some support to theism. The only reason which Nielsen gives for rejecting this claim is, so far as I can see, that the situation so described is compatible with a sceptical interpretation. In other words the sceptic could, without contradicting himself, continue to maintain that he was experiencing no more than a set of highly surprising natural

13

phenomena, notwithstanding the fact that his present situation coincides very closely with what theists had always predicted and is totally different from what atheists had expected.

This is, of course, true. Unless the experiences jointly entail the truth of the theistic interpretation, the truth of the atheistic interpretation remains a logical possibility. But to insist that theism would be put beyond reasonable doubt only if its truth were entailed by the truth of the factual statements which support it is to employ a criterion which Nielsen has already, rightly, rejected in his discussion of phenomenalism [16]. There he recognises that a statement about a material object may be confirmed beyond reasonable doubt, although it is not entailed by the sense-datum statements that support it. Those sense-datum statements are compatible with the denial of the material object statement in the sense that it remains logically possible that the latter might be false. Nielsen's suggestion that the difference between the theist's and the atheist's interpretation of Hick's post-mortem experiences might be 'purely verbal' exactly parallels the claim that used to be made by logical positivists that the difference between realists and phenomenalists about perception was purely verbal, a claim which Ayer has since abandoned [17].

A possible objection to my description in non-theistic terms of the situation to which Hick appeals as affording an eschatological verification of Christian claims is that it introduces experiences which are not sense-experiences. Jesus is represented in it as highly numinous. Nielsen might wish to say that such 'evidence' is not allowable. The passage in which he discusses the appeal to religious (or, more specifically, mystical) experience is of great interest for the whole of the present issue. He embarks upon it in reply to the charge that Ayer's formulation of the verification principle is too restrictive in that, for purposes of verification, it limits possible experience to sense-experience, and thus fails to take account of the evidential role of religious experience [18]. Nielsen himself does not, in fact, wish to restrict experience in this way, but maintains that mystical experience is neutral

14

as between theistic and non-theistic interpretations. This in itself is not surprising; it is what one would expect him to say in the light of his general views on the verifiability of religious claims. Mystical experience, whatever its character, will necessarily be such as to be compatible with a non-theistic interpretation, for such an interpretation will always be logically possible. Hence a difference between theist and atheist as to its interpretation will be purely verbal.

The interesting and significant thing is, however, that Nielsen's very careful discussion of this question does not proceed on these predictable lines at all. Instead he pays close attention to the actual character of the experience in so far as it can be separated from the very various interpretations placed upon it by mystics reared in different traditions. He concludes, on the basis of this scrutiny, that the experience in itself does not support any single interpretation rather than any other, and that it is, in this sense, 'religiously and theologically neutral' [19]. It is implied in his whole treatment of this question that the answer might have been different; the nature of mystical experience might, on investigation, have turned out to be such as distinctly to favour one interpretation rather than another. Unless this possibility was present, there was no need to attend carefully to the facts; their irrelevance could have been presumed in advance. This means that the argument from religious experience (which I shall consider briefly in the next chapter) is treated by Nielsen as in principle legitimate, and dispute between theists and atheists will rightly involve the sort of scrutiny of actual experiences which Nielsen has briefly undertaken and which such writers as R. C. Zaehner, Ninian Smart and W. T. Stace have engaged in more fully [20]. This being so, there can be no objection to my including in my description a numinous experience of an unambiguous kind.

The theistic statements that philosophers generally discuss are, as Nielsen says, comparatively remote from the periphery of the theistic system, so that they are not immediately sensitive to differences in what is observed. This is true of Nielsen's usual example, 'God governs the world', but, as will become clear in our later discussion, this is a feature which is

15

common to scientific, political and religious systems [21]. It does not mean that the system as a whole is immune to all experiential test.

The contention that theism is logically incoherent because God cannot be identified must rely on some general thesis about the requirements for identifying *anything*, requirements which it is claimed cannot be satisfied in the case of God. The argument is clearly stated by S. N. Hampshire [22]:

> An atheist . . . may know very well what a particular set of theological propositions means, and he may know by what tests true statements about the properties of God are conventionally distinguished from false statements; he may be able to describe the conventionally accepted criteria of application for theological expressions, and he may be able to explain what ordinarily counts as sufficient evidence that a theological statement of this type is true. But he may still believe that no statement of this type about God can be accepted as true, in the last analysis, on the grounds that the conventionally accepted criteria of application attached to the subject-term, violate some more general requirements which any such criteria of application should satisfy. He may hold, for example, that it is illegitimate to refer to God as the subject of a statement in the manner required, since nothing would properly count as identifying God, and nothing would properly count as distinguishing him from other things; and he might hold that there is some universal and necessary connection between the possibility of identification and of individuation and a claim to existence.

Ordinarily, if we are called upon to explain what we are talking about we either direct the hearer's attention to the object in question, if it is present to him, or we provide a description of it which is full enough to enable him to recognise it. Ideally, we provide a unique description, i.e., one which applies to what we are talking about and to

16

nothing else. When we can indicate or point to the thing we generally rely on the context to make clear what it is in the area indicated to which we are referring, and it may be necessary to help the process with some description. We can, in any case, never rule out entirely the possibility of the hearer's getting it wrong and failing to recognise what it is that we are talking about. But, given a full enough description and a reasonably receptive hearer, successful reference can normally be achieved.

Why, then, we might ask, can we not make clear what we are talking about, in the case of God, by providing a description which applies uniquely to him: 'The Creator of heaven and earth', 'Almighty and Everlasting God' (the Collects in the Book of Common Prayer afford many examples which would seem to satisfy the requirement)? It is clear that Hampshire does not regard this as enough, nor does Nielsen who is similarly puzzled about the possibility of identifying God [23]. Hampshire's reason for discounting the possibility of providing an identifying reference for 'God' through one or more unique descriptions appears to be that such descriptions are not enough unless it is also possible to indicate what we are talking about in some non-verbal way. Thus he objects to talk of 'vast impersonal forces in history' on the ground that there are no situations to which we can point and say 'here is one of the vast impersonal forces'. But, as Nielsen recognises, such a requirement is much too restrictive and would exclude such theoretical terms in science as 'electric field of force' or 'Schrödinger wave function'; and, one might add, numbers, time, mental images, the universe itself [24]. Nielsen at this point virtually abandons the claim that identifying God represents a separate problem and is content to argue, in the manner we have already considered, that, although God might in principle be identified through unique descriptions, in fact the predicates which appear in such descriptions cannot be given a determinate meaning. The problem of identifying God collapses into the problem of verifying statements about him.

Nevertheless there does seem to be a problem as to whether and, if so, how our normal devices for making clear

17

what we are talking about can be applied in the case of God. When we are talking about a particular entity, we can indeed normally make clear to our hearer what entity it is either by indicating it or by providing a description which applies only to it. However, the only way in which he can be sure that there is not some other entity of the same kind answering to the same description is by relating the entity in some unique way to the hearer's position here and now. Pointing does this automatically but, if that is not possible (as is the case with unobservable sub-microscopic particles in physics), it is necessary to be able to show how the entity is related to the hearer in space and time. This is what the believer in 'vast and impersonal forces in history' is unable to do and what, it is claimed, the believer in God is unable to do.

When the problem is set out in this way, it becomes clear that the usual means of identifying reference cannot apply to God, for he is not in space and, if he is in time, he is in all time. God, as theologians often say, is not 'one entity among others'. There is, therefore, no question of making clear which (spatio-temporal) entity is being talked about when God is the subject of discourse. There is no need, in his case, to 'pick him out' from among other entities of the same kind, since there are no other entities of the same kind. This does not mean that it is impossible to point to instances of divine activity in the spatio-temporal world. As we have seen, there are criteria which can, at least in principle, be used to enable us to discern such activity. Nor does it mean that there is no sense in which 'God' can be ostensively defined, for, if traditional Christian theism is true, there are men who have been aware of the presence of God [25]. But it does mean that the only way in which God can be distinguished from other subjects of discourse is by reference to his distinguishing characteristics. If these are in themselves intelligible and consistent with one another, they define a transcendent being who, as such, is distinguishable from any other kind of entity. Whether there exists a transcendent being with these distinguishing characteristics is, of course, a different issue altogether, but to deny his existence on the sole ground that, if he existed, he would constitute an exception to the manner

18

in which we normally provide identifying references, is to beg the question against the theist by demanding that theism accommodate itself to an essentially atheistical metaphysic.

There remains a problem about the meaning of predicates as applied to God which is largely independent of the issue of verifiability. It concerns the possibility of giving a determinate meaning to expressions like 'father', 'loving', 'wise' when they are used of God, given that these words and others like them are normally used of human beings who are finite. It is customary to say that they are used 'analogically' of God, so that only some of the implications of their ordinary use carry over to their use in a theological context. The difficulty then is to tell how much of the original meaning remains.

The answer would seem to be that a word should be presumed to carry with it as many of the original entailments as the new context allows, and this is determined by their compatibility with the other descriptions which there is reason to believe also apply to God. That God is incorporeal dictates that 'father' does not mean 'physical progenitor', but the word continues to bear the connotation of tender protective care. Similarly God's 'wisdom' is qualified by the totality of other descriptions which are applicable to him; it does not, for example, have to be learned, since he is omniscient and eternal. There is, in principle, no difference between this procedure and that which is followed in the sciences, where a similar problem arises. When words like 'particle' and 'wave' are used of entities which are not directly observable, they are used analogically and must be presumed to bear only so much of their ordinary meaning as is compatible with the theories which govern their use.

In the foregoing discussion a certain pattern has emerged. The philosophical critic of theism attempts to forestall any positive arguments in its favour by calling attention to some general requirement of logic which, he claims, it violates. The philosophical defender of theism replies that the critique fails in one or other of two ways: either it is based on a misunderstanding of theism, or it involves metaphysical assumptions which the theist is prepared to challenge. The

19

critic, in his turn, will presumably have to contend that the theist is necessarily committed to formulating theism in the ways that have been criticised; and that his own metaphysical assumptions are to be preferred to those of the theist. Along these lines the dispute can and does continue, but it is no longer possible to avoid an examination of the positive case for theism.

2 Can God's Existence be Proved?

Whether belief in God can be shown to be necessarily false requires much more thorough discussion than I have been able to give it. The considerations advanced in the previous chapter are, I suggest, sufficient to justify the assumption that it has not yet been done.

A further possibility, which has to be taken with equal seriousness, is that the existence of God can be demonstrated or, at any rate, shown to be probable in some strict sense of that word [1]. It is at first sight surprising that it should have been claimed both that theism can be conclusively refuted and that it can be conclusively demonstrated; but we need to bear in mind the subtlety and complexity of the issues and the enormous difficulty of making explicit the grounds of deep conviction.

There is, however, one standpoint from which the situation ceases to appear paradoxical, that of those who regard the ontological argument as the key to the whole problem. Thus Norman Malcolm writes [2]:

> What Anselm proved is that the notion of contingent existence or of contingent non-existence cannot have any application to God. His existence must either be logically necessary or logically impossible. The only intelligible way of rejecting Anselm's claim that God's existence is necessary is to maintain that the concept of God as a being greater than which cannot be conceived, is self-contradictory or nonsensical.

That is to say, if God is by definition a being whose existence is logically necessary, if he does *not* exist, it can

21

only be because, as Findlay argued [3], it is logically impossible that there should be a being whose existence is logically necessary.

Malcolm distinguishes two forms of the argument which he thinks Anselm did not clearly differentiate. The alternatives are most clearly discernible in Descartes' formulation of the argument, where he says that 'it is in truth necessary for me to assert that God exists after having presupposed that he possesses every sort of perfection, since existence is one of these' [4]. To talk in this way of existence as a 'perfection' is to imply that it is a characteristic whose possession by a thing alters its nature; so that, for example, one could compare a house which does not yet exist with the same house as later existing and judge the latter 'better' or 'more perfect' simply because it exists and although, as built, it differs in no way from the architect's specification. It is this assumption which Kant identified as the fallacy underlying the ontological argument, the fallacy of holding that 'existence is a predicate' [5]:

by whatever and by however many predicates we may think a thing — even if we completely determine it — we do not make the least addition to the thing when we further declare that this thing *is*. Otherwise it would not be exactly the same thing that exists, but something more than we had thought in the concept; and we could not therefore say that the exact object of my concept exists.

The denial that existence is, in any sense, a predicate has been criticised [6] but, as Hick has pointed out: 'The issue . . . is not whether 'exists' functions as a predicate in *any* sense, but whether it functions as the kind of predicate that the ontological argument requires it to be' [7].

Malcolm accepts that existence is not a perfection, and is, therefore, not a predicate of the kind required, but maintains that *necessary* existence is a perfection. And it is on this claim that the second version of the argument turns. Of Anselm he remarks: 'His first ontological proof uses the principle that a thing is greater if it exists than if it does not

22

exist. His second proof employs the different principle that a thing is greater if it necessarily exists than if it does not necessarily exist' [8]. It is evident that this form of the argument can succeed only if God's existing necessarily is taken to mean that it is logically necessary that there should be a God — or logically impossible that there should not be. If the necessary being of God is interpreted in any other way it will continue to be an open question whether there is a necessary being so interpreted. But if, as Malcolm has already conceded, to say of something that it exists, when this means simply that there is such a thing, is not to ascribe a predicate to it, to say that it exists necessarily, when 'exists' is used in the same sense, is not to ascribe a predicate to it either. That is to say that necessary existence, so interpreted, is not a perfection, because the concept is incoherent.

To put the point in a different way. We can, if we choose, so define God as to make it true by definition that God exists; it then follows that nothing is God unless it exists. But our doing this cannot decide the question whether there is anything corresponding to our definition. If we now attempt to close this question by modifying our definition so as to make it true by definition that God necessarily exists, it still remains an open question whether there is anything answering to this definition. If 'necessarily' here means 'by logical necessity', we can indeed be sure that nothing exists answering to the definition, for nothing can. The matter is well summed up by Shaffer [9]:

We are thus led to the result that the Ontological Argument of itself alone cannot show the existence of God, in the sense in which the concept is shown to have extension. And this is just as the religious wish it to be. They do not conceive of God as something whose being expresses itself entirely in the concepts and propositions of a language game. They conceive of Him as something which has effects on the world and can in some way be experienced. Here is a crucial respect in which his status is meant to be different from that of the numbers. The concept of God is a concept which *might* have extension.

23

But some further argument is required to show whether it does or not.

The language of necessity as applied to God is, nevertheless, characteristic of traditional Christian theism, and part of the attraction of the ontological argument is due to a conviction that necessity of some sort is involved in the idea of God. Thus Malcolm in endeavouring to explain 'necessary existence' writes [10]:

Some remarks about the notion of *dependence* may help to make this latter principle intelligible. Many things depend for their existence on other things and events. My house was built by a carpenter: its coming into existence was dependent on a certain creative activity. Its continued existence is dependent on many things: that a tree does not crush it, that it is not consumed by fire, and so on. If we reflect on the common meaning of the word 'God' (no matter how vague and confused this is), we realise that it is incompatible with this meaning that God's existence should *depend* on anything. Whether we believe in him or not, we must admit that the 'almighty and everlasting God' (as several ancient prayers begin), the 'Maker of heaven and earth, and of all things visible and invisible' (as is said in the Nicene Creed), cannot be thought of as being brought into existence by anything or as depending for his continued existence on anything. To conceive of anything as dependent upon something else for its existence is to conceive of it as a lesser being than God.

In saying that God is, in this sense, unconditioned and independent Malcolm is no longer employing the notion of logical necessity. This idea of a God upon whom all things depend, but who himself depends on nothing, is associated with the cosmological argument rather than the ontological. The argument proceeds from the world to God, and claims that the universe requires explanation and can be explained only as the product of a divine Creator. As an attempt at demonstration it is exposed to a dilemma: if everything

24

requires explanation, God himself requires explanation; if, however, not everything requires explanation – if there must be some brute facts – why should not the universe be a brute fact which requires no explanation? To the atheist it seems evident that there is no need for an explanation of the universe and that the concept of a self-explanatory being is logically incoherent [11].

A way of avoiding this dilemma might be to relax the requirement that everything should be explained and claim simply that explanations should be sought wherever possible. The theist can then maintain that the world is capable of being explained as the product of a divine Creator and that such an explanation is to be preferred to none at all. He is no longer exposed to the objection that God himself must be explained, since he is not now committed to the necessity of explaining everything. Explanation must indeed stop somewhere, but it stops where explanation is no longer needed, not with a being that is self-explanatory [12].

On this view of the matter it is open to the theist to venture the hypothesis that the world was created by God, but the atheist need not accept the need for any such hypothesis. It follows that the cosmological argument, on this interpretation, does not prove the existence of God; nor is the hypothesis a scientific hypothesis, which can be rendered more or less probable. There is no room for the comparison of similar instances which is the basis of inductive reasoning, since there is only one universe.

Hick concludes his assessment of the argument, which has proceeded along similar lines, by claiming that it leaves the alternatives open. The atheist, he believes, can accept the possibility of the theistic interpretation, but

having agreed that the universe is either unexplained or to be explained theistically, he would add that there is no reason here to adopt the latter alternative. There is no adequate reason to do other than accept the universe as simply an ultimate inexplicable datum. For whilst the cosmological argument presents us with the options: universe as brute fact or as divine creation, it does not provide any ground for preferring one to the other [13].

25

The atheist is in fact unlikely to accept this eirenic proposal. Antony Flew, for example, states what he calls 'the Stratonician presumption' [14]:

> the presumption, defeasible of course by adverse argument, must be that all qualities observed in things are qualities belonging by natural right to those things themselves; and hence that whatever characteristics we think ourselves able to discern in the universe as a whole are the underivative characteristics of the universe itself.

This presumption, which provides a reason for preferring the atheistic alternative, is simply a special case of the demand for economy; and there is an obvious sense in which atheism is more economical than theism. On the other hand, if a theistic explanation is admissible at all, theism can carry explanation further than atheism and this too is, so far as it goes, a theoretical advantage.

There is, however, a further reason why the atheist is unwilling to allow that a theistic explanation is admissible. He contends, in the manner of Kant, that such concepts as 'cause' or 'explanation' are intelligible only within the natural world and lose their sense when a cause or explanation is sought of the natural world itself. This contention represents a particular application of the general thesis [15] that the predicates ascribed to God cannot be given a determinate sense because, when used of God, they are removed from the context which provides their ordinary meaning. Thus when God is spoken of as 'first cause', the word 'cause' is not used in the same sense as it is when we speak of a fire causing smoke.

This criticism compels us to take a fresh look at the entire discussion. The cosmological argument, as traditionally presented, presupposes that a request for explanation is always appropriate and that in order to explain the existence of the world a causal explanation is required. Critics of the argument insist that explanation of the world's existence, if it involves postulating God, cannot stop at that point; and that a causal explanation cannot, in any case, terminate in a transcendent 'first cause'. There is evidently room for misunderstanding between the disputants both about the sort of explanation they have in mind and about the sort of cause.

Smart takes the initial step towards removing these misunderstandings when he points out that the explanation which the theist offers involves postulating that the universe is due to an act of pure creativity on the part of a transcendent being whose nature is personal. This makes clear that it is a causal explanation of a different kind from that which is customary in the sciences. It does not rely on general laws established by the observation of many instances. It is analogous to the sort of explanation provided when events are viewed as the actions of conscious agents. The effect of such an explanation is to render the event intelligible in an entirely new way by providing a framework of interpretation different from, and not reducible to, the scientific. The metaphysical explanation which the theist offers does, however, resemble scientific explanation in two important respects:

(i) The explanatory hypothesis is arrived at by an imaginative leap. It is not deducible from the facts which it purports to explain.

(ii) It seeks to explain not a single set of phenomena, but a whole range of different phenomena.

An explanation of this type is not exposed to the original dilemma. Any metaphysical system, like any scientific system, will employ certain ultimate categories in terms of which everything else is to be explained. To complain that, unless these are explained also, nothing is explained is to misunderstand the nature of such explanations. The question to be decided when rival explanatory schemes confront one another is which set of ultimate categories is to be preferred [16]. Whether such a question can in principle be answered is the subject of Part II of this book.

What has been said about the role of the cosmological argument suggests that it needs to be taken in conjunction with the teleological argument and the argument from religious experience. The teleological argument was in the seventeenth and eighteenth centuries widely influential in a

27

form which was severely criticised by Hume and has since then been rendered obsolete by the theory of natural selection. There is, nevertheless, a version of the argument which is less easily disposed of, the argument from the kind and degree of order in the universe. The 'order' which prompts the argument is of two sorts:

(i) There is the fact that the universe is not chaotic, although it might have been. It obeys scientific laws and affords regularities of the kind that are needed for it to be the subject of thought and language. It seems, on the face of it, vastly improbable that it should just happen to be so.

(ii) There is, further, the evolutionary development whereby the universe not only manifests the sort of regularity which science discovers, but has produced rational beings with the capacity to think and love and worship.

As Austin Farrer puts it, it is hard to credit that an original mindless collocation of atoms 'had it in it' to produce all this [17].

As Smart points out, the distinction between order and chaos is less straightforward than it looks at first sight. Suppose, for instance, we think of chaos as an 'enormous quantity of atoms buzzing about in a random way':

Even such a universe would be organised a bit: for if there were no stability or regularity whatsoever, how could we single out individual atoms? True disorderliness — absolute disorderliness — would be utter chaos; but here we could no longer speak of this, that or the next thing. In effect there would be no cosmos. Nothingness and absolute chaos would be indistinguishable [18].

This presents a problem for the theist. Is he to say that any degree of order — any cosmos — provides reason for postulating the God of traditional Christian theism, so that even Smart's 'enormous quantity of atoms buzzing about in a random way' would do so? Or should he say that it is the actual cosmos, with the kind and degree of order that it has which requires a divine orderer? This is the solution which Smart proposes: 'The teleological argument, then, has to

28

begin with more than the fact of orderliness if it wishes to infer an intelligent Author of nature' [19].

The existence of this difficulty affords a further reason for abandoning the habit of treating the traditional arguments as separate inferences terminating in a single entity, which leaves one with the further problem of showing that it is the same entity which is required by each of the arguments. A very rudimentary universe of the kind Smart envisages would support, at best, only a very rudimentary and indeterminate form of theism.

The teleological argument has not usually been put forward as a proof of God's existence. Indeed its attractiveness has consisted in its claim to be an empirical argument. It is as such that it was treated with respect by Hume and finally rejected by him on the ground, among others, that it does not conform to the requirements of 'experimental reasoning concerning matter of fact and existence'. The objection is concisely stated by Flew. If someone asks how there can be so much order without design:

> We ... ask: 'How does he know what is probable or improbable about universes?' For his question ... presupposes that he knows something which not merely does he not know, but which neither he nor anyone else conceivably ever could know. No one could acquire an experience of universes to give him the necessary basis for this sort of judgement of probability or improbability; for the decisive reason that there could not be universes to have experience of [20].

Hick, summing up a similar discussion, concludes: 'What these considerations show is that any notion of probability properly invoked by a comprehensive teleological argument must be other than the usual statistical or logical concept' [21].

We may accept this judgement without at the same time concluding that the argument is without weight. It is an argument from analogy and, as such, escapes Flew's criticism; for the analogy to which it appeals is not between this and

29

other universes (which he rightly takes to be absurd), but between the universe as a whole and other ordered systems within it [22]. The criticisms which Hume and others have directed against the argument lose much of their point, if it is not taken as providing an entirely independent and sufficient method of establishing the existence and nature of God.

The arguments considered so far belong to what is traditionally called 'natural theology'. While they continue to engage the interest of philosophers, theologians have tended to neglect them and to appeal instead to religious experience and revelation. The argument from religious experience has a particular attraction for those who are dissatisfied with the metaphysical character of natural theology and who are impressed by the phenomenon of religion as a pervasive feature of human culture. It seems to do justice to its uniqueness while at the same time satisfying the demand for a science of religion. Moreover in speaking of a God who can, in some sense, be known directly, it is closer to ordinary religious belief and practice than are the traditional proofs. Indeed the traditional arguments themselves have often been interpreted as expressing a fundamental intuition misleadingly cast in the forms of logical inference.

That there is such a thing as religious experience and that it is phenomenologically distinct from other kinds of experience is strongly suggested by a study of such works as William James's 'Varieties of Religious Experience' and Rudolf Otto's 'Idea of the Holy'. The title of James's book calls attention to something which Otto tended to overlook: that religious experiences are of many different kinds. Otto has comparatively little to say about mystical experience (which Nielsen, as we have seen, treats as if it were the only kind of religious experience) and concentrates on what he calls 'the sense of the numinous'. The experience is, characteristically, that of being confronted by something of immense significance and majesty which is other than oneself and not to be identified with any other constituent of the natural world. Characteristically, also, the experience presents itself as 'self-authenticating'. The individual who undergoes it cannot doubt the reality of that which he encounters.

The problems arise when the attempt is made to give a rational account of the experience. It is notoriously difficult to separate the experience from the interpretations placed upon it, so as to decide whether it favours one interpretation rather than another. If it is claimed that the experience is self-authenticating, we need to ask what this means. Does it mean no more than that the individual who has it cannot be mistaken about the felt quality of the experience? This, even if true (and it can be disputed), does not entitle him to pronounce with certainty upon the nature or even the existence of the being that he purports to encounter. If it be granted that he is aware of something 'wholly other', can he infer from the experience itself that the 'wholly other' is the Creator of heaven and earth, the judge of all men [23]? The possibility cannot be ruled out of an alternative explanation in physiological or psychological terms.

In this connection, too, as with the arguments of natural theology, no satisfactory solution is to be found by relaxing the stringency of the claim and substituting probability for proof. For how could one estimate the degree of probability that an experience represents a genuine encounter with God when one is not in a position to compare the experiences in question with others that are known to be experiences of God?

Nevertheless it would seem to be unwarranted dogmatism to deny such experiences any evidential value. As we have seen, Nielsen is led by his scrutiny of mystical experience to conclude that it is, in fact, neutral as between theistic and non-theistic interpretations. It seems likely that a similar scrutiny of numinous experiences would find them to accord better with theism [24]. What is needed is a careful study of the evidence. To argue that, because alternative interpretations are possible, no single interpretation is to be preferred to any other, is either to fall into Nielsen's fallacy of failing to distinguish between logical possibility and positive support or to embrace the thesis that the description of such experiences is wholly determined by the beliefs of those who have them. The paradoxical nature of this thesis is well

31

brought out by Smart [25]:

> ... it would be indeed odd if metaphysics, considered as
> sets of propositions to be entertained and believed by
> people, should have the enormous effect of creating out of
> nothing the powerful religious experiences of both great
> teachers and ordinary folk. It is easier to explain a dualism
> between God and the soul by reference to the experience
> of prophets and worshippers than to explain the latter by
> reference to a current doctrine of dualism.

The 'proofs' so far discussed are of a very general kind and
pertain to theism rather than to specifically Christian theism.
For this reason they have sometimes been treated with
suspicion by Christian theologians who wish to emphasise the
uniqueness of the Judaeo-Christian tradition, which lies in its
historical claims. The 'biblical theology' which has been so
influential in this century appeals to the acts of God in
history rather than to what are felt to be abstract philosophical arguments. The earliest Christian preaching took as
its central message the resurrection of Jesus from the dead
and the dominant theme of the Bible, and so of biblical
theology, is God's saving acts. As G. E. Wright expresses it:
'To be sure there is an immediate awareness of God's
presence in worship, prayer, communion, confession, but the
main emphasis of the Bible is certainly on his revelation of
himself in historical acts and in definite "words", not in
diffuse experience' [26].
    It is characteristic of biblical theology that it regards
revelation as a source, perhaps the only source, of knowledge
about God; or, if that is too philosophical a way of putting it,
it regards 'because it is revealed in and through the events
recorded in the Bible' as a sufficient answer to the question,
'Why do you believe?'
    Although there is at present something of a reaction
against biblical theology among theologians, it can scarcely
be denied that the Christian Church has traditionally believed
that God has revealed himself uniquely in the history of the
Jewish people and in the life, death and resurrection of Jesus,
    32

and that the Bible is an essential witness to these events.

The objections to such reliance upon the biblical narratives in support of the dogmatic claims of Christianity are of two kinds. The first kind is general and theoretical. Historical research yields conclusions which are, at best, tentative and open to revision. In-so-far, therefore, as Christian theism is based upon history, it cannot achieve certainty. Moreover it is impossible for historical research to discover the sort of facts which are involved in the crucial instances of God's action in history, such as the resurrection of Jesus. Even if it is conceded, as it would not be by some, that such a miraculous event could have occurred, it is logically impossible that there should be sufficient historical evidence to warrant belief in its occurrence. The argument (classically and, some would say, definitively set out by Hume) is from the presuppositions of scientific history. According to it the historian is bound to assume that the same sorts of causes will operate at one time or place as at another. If he were to admit the possibility of divine interventions in the course of history, he would be unable to fit them into any scheme of rational interpretation. The most he can do in support of a miraculous claim is to admit that there is something that he cannot fully or satisfactorily explain.

Moreover — and this is the second kind of objection — the actual investigations of biblical scholars cast doubt on some of the assumptions which are needed to justify the conclusions of biblical theology. The Bible, even the New Testament alone, is the work of many writers, often differing in their aims and assumptions and sometimes in plain disagreement with each other. There is much controversy as to the historical value of the various parts of it and it is difficult, if not impossible, to distinguish historical fact from theological interpretation. The Bible, as presented by the biblical critics, is unsuited to be a vehicle of divine revelation in anything like the traditional sense.

Even if these objections can to some extent be met, as I believe they can [27], they are enough to show that historical research alone cannot validate a claim to revelation, nor can such a claim be established without reference to

33

historical research. It follows that revelation cannot of itself afford proof of God's existence or render it probable in any strict sense.

Some theologians have sought to retain the emphasis upon the primacy of the Bible, while avoiding the difficulties about scientific history, by distinguishing between secular and sacred history and treating the biblical narratives as exercises in the latter. Understood in this way they provide us with ultimate categories in terms of which to interpret all human experience. This proposal is not, however, offered as a means of proving Christian doctrine; rather it is suggested that, in such a fundamental matter as our entire understanding of life, proof is out of place and we must be content to be guided by presuppositions, which determine for us what shall count as proof. This whole approach to the question of religion I shall consider later [28].

The discussion, in this chapter and the preceding one, of the various ways in which it has been attempted to demonstrate or render it probable that the God of Christian theism exists or to show that the idea of such a God is logically incoherent, is bound to have aroused dissatisfaction in serious believers or, for that matter, in serious unbelievers. This is partly because the treatment has had to be summary and schematic, omitting all the detail and all the nuances which might have helped to make the arguments persuasive. It is hard not to feel that we have been through a series of intellectual exercises which are somewhat remote from the considerations which really prompt men to belief or unbelief. Why this should be so will, I hope, emerge at a later stage in the argument. However, so far as it has been able to go, the outcome of our survey would appear to be that all such attempts have failed.

If this is so, there would seem to remain only two possibilities:

(i) Religion is not capable of rational assessment in any straightforward sense. The individual has ultimately to make an existential choice, unsupported by reasons, for or against religious belief.

(ii) It is, indeed, possible to make a rational case for and

34

against a system of religious belief, but it is a case which relies on a set of interrelated arguments, which do not conform to the ordinary pattern of deductive or inductive reasoning.

Part II

3 The Nature of a Cumulative Case

The purpose of Part I was to justify, in an admittedly summary fashion, two assumptions which will be made in the remainder of the book. They are that it is not possible to prove traditional Christian theism or to render it probable in any strict sense of the word; and that it cannot be shown to be necessarily false or logically incoherent.

Only two alternatives would seem to remain: either (i) there can be no rational case for or against Christianity, or (ii) the case must be a cumulative one which is rational, but does not take the form of a strict proof or argument from probability. In what follows I shall be concerned only with whether Christian belief may be rationally defended and, if so, in what way. My intention is not to provide such a defence but to consider how, if at all, it might be provided and, in so doing, to give an account of the nature of the disagreement between theists and atheists that might commend itself to both parties.

Among the reasons, both philosophical and theological, for denying that there can be a rational case for Christianity the most influential has been the assumption that any argument, to be rational, must conform to the requirements of proof or strict probability. The contention of the present chapter will be that the assumption in question is false. In it I shall endeavour to show that in fields other than theology we commonly, and justifiably, make use of arguments other than those of proof or strict probability; and that, typically, theological arguments are of this kind.

What has been taken to be a series of failures when treated as attempts at purely deductive or inductive argument could well be better understood as contributions to a cumulative

39

case. On this view the theist is urging that traditional Christian theism makes better sense of all the evidence available than does any alternative on offer, and the atheist is contesting the claim. The dispute concerns what Gilbert Ryle calls 'the plausibility of theories' [1] rather than proof or probability in any strict sense.

There is an obvious danger in this suggestion, noted with pleasing asperity by Flew [2]:

> Nor, incidentally, will it do to recognize that of a whole series of arguments each individually is defective, but then to urge that nevertheless in sum they comprise an impressive case; perhaps adding as a sop to the Cerberus of criticism that this case is addressed to the whole personality and not merely to the philosophical intellect. We have here to insist upon a sometimes tricky distinction: between, on the one hand, the valid principle of the accumulation of evidence, where every item has at least some weight in its own right; and, on the other hand, the Ten-leaky-buckets-Tactic, applied to arguments none of which hold water at all. The scholarly and the businesslike procedure is to examine arguments one by one, without pretending — for no better reason than that they have been shown to be mistaken — that clearly and respectably stated contentions must be other than they are.

It is indeed an error to construe as the constituents of a cumulative case what are in fact properly to be understood as entirely separate and invalid arguments, but until it has been shown either that cumulative arguments of the kind envisaged are not possible or that the theistic case is not an instance of one, Flew's warning must remain no more than a salutary reminder of possible risks.

Prima facie the elements of the theistic scheme do tend to reinforce one another in a way that is recognisable both by theists and by their opponents. Thus, although the cosmological and teleological arguments do not (if our criticism of them was correct) prove that there must be a transcendent creator of the world, they do make explicit one way

40

(arguably the best way) in which the existence and nature of the universe can be explained, if indeed they can be explained at all. The atheist is entitled, as we saw, to deny that the universe requires explanation, and so long as the matter is left there, the theist's far-ranging claims can rest on nothing more than the abstract consideration that explanation is to be sought wherever possible. But when there is brought into the reckoning the claim of some men to be aware of the presence of God, and of others to have witnessed the action of God in the world or to have been addressed by him, the case is altered. These claims cannot simply be dismissed without reason given. It is true that the sense of the presence of God (for example) involves an element of interpretation and can consistently be interpreted otherwise by the atheist. Nevertheless it can reasonably be demanded of any interpretation that it deal adequately with the phenomenon in its fullest and most impressive forms, in which it has been so strong and so pervasive of a man's entire life that he himself, at least, could scarcely doubt the reality of his encounter with God. How others should judge it may properly depend on its effects on the individual's life. If, as tends to happen, it informs a character of unusual charity and strength, or effects a transformation into such a character, it becomes correspondingly hard even for the uncommitted to withold the name of saint. The word can be used, as it were in inverted commas, in such a way as to admit the presence of certain rare qualities while denying the man's own ascription of them to the grace of God. But to use it in this way, notwithstanding the individual's own testimony, requires some justification, which would have to be in terms of some non-theistic world view, for which conspicuous sanctity must inevitably pose a problem, associated as it is, on such a view, with manifest error.

In dismissing the saint's account of his own activity and experience it is not enough to claim merely that alternative explanations are possible: it is necessary to produce them or, at least, to indicate in some detail what they might be like. If psychological or sociological theories are invoked to explain why the testimony of the saints is to be regarded as suspect,

41

these must be considered on their merits. It will not do for the theist to argue that, if the saints are sane, their testimony cannot be rejected [3], for they may have been systematically misled by a cultural tradition which encouraged them (as we can now see) to misconstrue their experience. Nevertheless, if they did in fact exemplify a quality of life of unusual power and grace of a kind or to a degree that their former personality gave no warrant for expecting, some weight attaches to their testimony that it was 'not I, but the grace of God that was with me', and the value to be given to it is necessarily related to whatever other reasons there may be for believing in the God whose character and purposes they purport to reflect [4]. The situation is analogous to that in which one man claims to have been influenced by another. In assessing his claim we pay attention to such matters as his general truthfulness, the contrast between his performance before and after the alleged influence, the extent to which his words and actions altered in conformity with the other's known views and whether the other was in a position to influence him. To the extent that we are satisfied by such tests as these we are the more inclined to trust his testimony; but his testimony makes its own independent contribution to our final judgement [5].

Again, the theist maintains, if there were a God who had created a universe in which there could develop rational beings capable of responding to him and to one another with love and understanding, it is to be anticipated that he would in some way communicate with them. The existence, then, of what purport to be such 'revelations' is something which tends to support the belief in a God who has in these ways revealed himself; although here too the support would be weakened if the historical and other evidence appealed to were to be seriously impugned, or if the concept of revelation were to run into intractable philosophical difficulties. That there is a variety of claims to be the revealed truth about God does not in itself show that none of the claims can be justified. We need to ask of each of them what sort of sense they make of human experience and of one another. It is also relevant to ask of each of them whether some other

42

interpretation, more satisfactory than is provided in its own terms, is available to explain its occurrence, its character and its effects.

The way in which the various elements in the Christian apologetic reinforce one another may, perhaps, be illustrated by a parable.

Two explorers find a hole in the ground, little more, perhaps, than a slight depression. One of them says, 'There is something funny about that hole; it doesn't look natural to me.' The other says, 'It's just an ordinary hole, and can be explained in a hundred and one different ways.' Shortly afterwards they come upon a number of smaller holes in the same area as the first. The first explorer thinks they must be related to it: indeed he fancies that they have the same *sort* of oddness about them. The other pooh-poohs the idea. He sees nothing in any way remarkable about the holes — anything could have caused them, they are probably just natural depressions. Later, to their surprise, they find in a neighbouring cave a papyrus containing fragments of the plan of a building. 'Ah,' says the first explorer, 'now I see what was odd about those holes; the big one was made to take the centre post of a wooden building, the smaller ones took the other posts.'

'All right,' says the other, 'we can soon test your theory. Let us take the fragments of your plan and piece them together on the site. If they fit, well and good, but they probably won't.' So they take them to the site. The first explorer says he can see how the plan fits the site, and arranges the fragments accordingly, with what might be the centre of the roof over the largest hole. Then he sketches his reconstruction out on paper and shows it to his companion. 'This is all very well,' says the latter, 'but you haven't accounted for *all* the holes or *all* the features shown in the fragments. The way the remainder fit is purely coincidental.' The first explorer replies that he doesn't claim to know precisely what the original building was like, or how all the details fitted in. Moreover he thinks he can explain why some of the features mentioned in the plan should be missing in what remains on the site. If his impression of the character of

43

the complete building is right, then these would be the first to be stolen or to disintegrate.

'But', says the other, 'the facts as we have them are compatible with a number of quite different interpretations. Each of them taken by itself can be explained away without much difficulty. And as for the fragmentary plan in the papyrus, of which you make such extensive use, it could well be an imaginative construction with no reference to the real world at all.'

In the parable the original large hole represents the intellectual demand for ultimate explanation to which natural theology appeals. The smaller holes represent private religious experiences of sin, grace, etc. The fragmentary plan represents the concepts of the Christian revelation.

I must make clear at once that the parable does not in any way claim to illuminate the problem of transcendence. To any such claim it might well be objected that the explorer when he notices something odd about the holes is unconsciously comparing them with other holes which he knows to have contained posts; but in the religious case there are no other experiences which are known to be experiences of God. At this point the analogy no longer serves [6]. What it is intended to represent, and what the present argument is concerned with, is the way in which the different considerations to which the Christian appeals may reinforce each other. No doubt the Christian case, like that of the explorer, would be more convincing in the eyes of its critics if everything could be fitted neatly into the pattern of the Christian revelation. But the Christian claims that, if the scheme is as he believes it to be, there is an irreducible element of mystery in it, and he would not expect, here and now, to be able to fit everything in.

If the considerations mentioned tend to co-operate in support of traditional Christian theism, it is equally clear that there are also serious arguments against it. Thus, although the existence and character of evil cannot be shown to be strictly incompatible with the creation of the world by an omnipotent and loving God, it does torture the faith of the believer more than any other circumstance and demands a

44

theodicy of some kind. The construction of such a theodicy may in turn expose the theist to philosophical attack – to the extent, for example, that it presupposes a belief in a life to come. And in so far as historical scholarship casts doubt on the central assertions of the Christian gospel, the entire fabric of traditional Christian belief is threatened. It is not, then, simply that the theist sees certain considerations as strengthening his case; he also sees other considerations as tending to weaken it. Nor, on the face of it, is it only from within the theist's own system of belief that these conflicting arguments are recognisable. The atheist, too, is able to appreciate that, for instance, conspicuous sanctity is a phenomenon which tells against his position, just as the existence of apparently gratuitous suffering argues for it. Each believes he can take care of objections to his position, or show how they can in principle be taken care of, but the need to do so makes it clear that they are indeed objections, which must be allowed to stand unless adequately met.

Thus the debate between theists and atheists is unlikely to make progress, so long as it is confined to a single argument, such as the cosmological argument, or, indeed, to a whole series of arguments, if these are to be taken piecemeal without at any stage being brought into relation to one another. Here, at least, the Cartesian strategy of 'dividing the question' must be resisted. The debate, to be useful, must take the form of a dialogue in which, as John Wisdom observes (in relation to a legal judgement), 'The process of argument is not a *chain* of demonstrative reasoning. It is a presenting and representing of those features of a case which severally co-operate in favour of the conclusion' [7]. In order to illustrate how such a dialogue proceeds it may be helpful to consider examples from disciplines other than theology. Two in particular suggest themselves: critical exegesis and history.

(i) *Critical Exegesis*
I have in mind here the endeavour to discover the meaning of a text. It may be a fairly extended passage or perhaps an entire work [8]. Notoriously scholars disagree about such

45

matters. How is the argument between them conducted, and is the argument rational? What commonly happens in a debate between scholars is that scholar A takes a certain passage to be the clue to the author's overall meaning. The sense of this passage seems to him quite obvious and also its importance in the work as a whole. However, he recognises that some other passages are on first reading difficult to reconcile with this one, as he has chosen to interpret it. So he has to bring these apparently recalcitrant passages into line by finding an interpretation of them which will fit; or, failing that, by conceding that they are discrepant, but dismissing the discrepancy as comparatively unimportant. If he can explain why these passages should be in this way discrepant (why Plato nodded *here*) so much the better. In extreme cases he may declare these passages spurious or emend the text; in that case he would benefit from some independent evidence on the point.

Scholar B, on the other hand, starts with a hunch that the key lies elsewhere, in a different passage from the one A relies upon. This passage he interprets differently from A and his overall exegesis based on it requires him also to interpret differently from A, A's own original passage.

Given these disagreements how should they proceed?

It might be thought that they should first try to reach agreement on which passage to start from; then try to agree on its meaning; and then consider what implications this has for the interpretation of the rest. It is obvious, I think, that this strategy will not work. B does not want to start from where A wants to start from. If he concedes this point, he has probably lost the argument already. So he tries to explain why he does not want to start from there: because, let us suppose, (*a*) the passage does not mean what A thinks it does, (*b*) to interpret the passage in the way A proposes and to give it the importance he claims for it distorts the overall interpretation.

B can hope to persuade A of (*b*) only by going through all the other relevant passages and comparing how they look on A's interpretation with how they look on his own. And this is, ultimately, the only way also in which he can hope to persuade A of (*a*). For part of his argument about the

46

meaning of this original passage will be that, if interpreted in A's manner, it will make nonsense or less good sense of some or all of the rest. In the end, then, A and B will need to take one another right through the text, and the argument will consist in each trying to convince the other of the need to give each passage the weight and significance that, in terms of his own interpretation, it ought to bear.

An illustration of this process may be found in the debate between Cleanth Brooks and Douglas Bush about the interpretation of Andrew Marvell's Horatian Ode [9]. The problem is to elucidate the attitude expressed in the poem to its subject, Cromwell. Brooks claims that 'from historical evidence alone we would suppose that the attitude towards Cromwell in this poem would have to be a complex one. And this complexity is reflected in the ambiguity of the compliments paid to him.' The poem begins:

> The forward youth that would appear
> Must now forsake his muses dear,
> Nor in the shadows sing
> His numbers languishing.

Brooks remarks that it is 'the "forward youth" whose attention the speaker directs to the example of Cromwell' and 'forward' may mean 'presumptuous', 'pushing' as well as 'high spirited', 'ardent', 'properly ambitious'. He then continues:

> The speaker, one observes, does not identify Cromwell himself as the 'forward youth', or say directly that Cromwell's career has been motivated by a striving for fame. But the implications of the first two stanzas do carry over to him. There is, for example, the important word 'so' to relate Cromwell to these stanzas:
>> So restless Cromwell could not cease . . .
> And 'restless' is as ambiguous in its meanings as 'forward', and in its darker connotations even more damning . . . .

Brooks goes on to develop an interpretation of the poem

47

according to which Cromwell is represented as a natural phenomenon 'like an elemental force — with as little will as the lightning bolt, and as little conscience'. The speaker is compelled to admire his energy as well as his virtues as a man, but it is a qualified admiration. For this is the man who

> Could by industrious valour climb
> To ruin the great work of time
> And cast the Kingdom old
> Into another mould.
> Though Justice against fate complain,
> And plead the ancient rights in vain:
> But those who hold or break
> As men are strong or weak.
> Nature that hateth emptiness
> Allows of penetration less:
> And therefore must make room
> Where greater spirits come.
> What field of all the Civil Wars
> Where his were not the deepest scars?

'The power achieved by Cromwell', he writes, 'is a forced power, a usurped power.'

Bush in his reply accuses Brooks of 'forcing the evidence to fit an unspoken assumption — namely, that a sensitive, penetrating, and well-balanced mind like Marvell could not really have admired a crude, single-minded, and ruthless man of action like Cromwell.' In his endeavour to substantiate this charge, he calls attention to passages in the poem which, taken in their ordinary, straightforward sense, do not bear the interpretation Brooks wishes to place upon them. Thus about the opening stanza he says:

> To the unprejudiced reader, the lines say that, in these troubled times, the young man of spirit must leave bookish and poetical pursuits for military action . . . The critic has already made up his mind about the poet's view of Cromwell, and, instead of taking 'forward' in its common and natural sense, must grasp at a pejorative possibility

48

(the meaning 'presumptuous', to judge from the New English Dictionary, has been commoner in modern times than it was in Marvell's).

He takes issue with Brooks similarly for his interpretation of 'restless'. But Bush fastens particularly on Brooks's treatment of a later passage:

The nature of Mr. Brooks's special pleading becomes conspicuous in his treatment of the next two lines, which are, for his problem, perhaps the most significant lines in the whole poem
'Tis madness to resist or blame
The force of angry Heaven's flame.
Mr. Brooks writes: 'Does the poet mean to imply that Charles has angered heaven — that he has merited his destruction? There is no suggestion that Cromwell is a thunderbolt hurled by an angry Jehovah — or even by an angry Jove. The general emphasis on Cromwell as an elemental force is thoroughly relevant here to counter this possible misreading. Certainly in the lines that follow there is nothing to suggest that Charles has angered heaven, or that the Justice which complains against his fate is anything less than justice.'
I do not know what to make of such a statement as 'There is no suggestion that Cromwell is a thunderbolt hurled by an angry Jehovah — or even by an angry Jove' since that is what Marvell unmistakably says . . . Mr. Brooks seems to be merely rejecting evidence that is signally inconvenient for his reading of the poem.

Even in this abbreviated summary, which inevitably does an injustice to the subtlety and complexity of the discussion, the pattern of the argument can be discerned. Guided by certain general assumptions, which Bush seeks to call in question, Brooks relies on certain stanzas in particular to support his overall interpretation and claims that certain others are ambiguous enough to admit of being construed in a manner consistent with it. Bush complains that these interpretations are forced and that the passages, taken in their natural sense, render Brooks's overall scheme more or less implausible. In like manner he goes on to insist that Brooks cannot adequately account for a passage in which Marvell appeals to Irish testimony on Cromwell's behalf.

There follows at once a passage that is probably more embarrassing than any other part of the ode to anyone intent upon proving that Marvell's main attitude toward Cromwell is hostility or at most unwilling respect for unscrupulous strength and courage:

And now the Irish are ashamed
To see themselves in one year tamed:
So much one man can do,
That does both act and know.
They can affirm his praises best,
And have, though overcome, confessed
How good he is, how just,
And fit for highest trust.

... Mr. Brooks is driven to what may be thought the desperate solution of finding the lines ironical, a view he thinks sanctioned by the earlier stanzas because the Irish have learned of the qualities in Cromwell that Marvell had praised, energy, activity, and the like. 'The Irish, indeed, are best able to affirm such praise as has been accorded to Cromwell; and they know from experience "how good he is, how just", for they have been blasted by the force of angry Heaven's flame, even as Charles has been.'

Since I cannot follow much of Mr. Brooks's reading of the earlier stanzas, I cannot follow such an explanation. Nothing in the wording seems to me to carry the faintest trace of irony; it is as straightforward a statement as we could have, however little we like it.

And so he concludes that 'the text of Marvell's poem means what it says ... the suggestion of irony raises a much more difficult problem, within the poem, than the one it seeks to explain'.

However, it is noteworthy that Bush himself cannot take

50

everything Marvell says entirely at its face value:

> Though Justice against Fate complain
> And plead the ancient rights in vain.

Here Bush in turn suggests an interpretation that is not, perhaps, the most obvious one, but which coheres with his overall position.

The word 'right' ('the ancient rights', 'his helpless right') may mean not only abstract rightness but traditional claims which may or may not be wholly right. 'Justice' may be absolute justice, or it may be the limited version of human law that must give way before divine will ('Fate', in Roman terms).

There is nothing improper in this. Given a range of possible meanings the critic is justified in selecting that meaning which, in the light of the poem as a whole (and any other relevant evidence), makes the best sense [10]. This is what both the disputants have done throughout, and the reader who wishes to judge between them has no option but to go carefully through the text giving full weight to all the considerations that have been advanced, and any others he can show to be relevant. The pattern of argument involved is that of which Newman wrote:

> It is the culmination of probabilities, independent of each other, arising out of the nature and circumstances of the case which is under review; probabilities too fine to avail separately, too subtle and circuitous to be convertible into syllogisms, too numerous and various for such conversion, even were they convertible [11].

(ii) *History*
A similar pattern is clearly discernible in much of historical controversy, most clearly, perhaps, in cases where the relevant evidence is comparatively restricted and, therefore, manageable. One thinks, in particular, of ancient history and

such celebrated conundrums as that of the termination of Caesar's command in Gaul — Mommsen's *'Rechtsfrage'*, which affects the legality of Caesar's crossing the Rubicon in 49 B.C. A recent reassessment of this problem by P. J. Cuff [12] exemplifies the way in which a historian can reinterpret a limited body of documentary evidence:

A bibliography running back to 1857 suggests irreconcilable evidence, disputed statements, a hopeless tangle of contradictions. Nothing new has emerged in the nature of ancient testimony. The problem remains what it has always been . . . My excuse for this paper is that it attempts to approach the question not through the notorious passages in Cicero's Letters but by a different route altogether. It is not a fresh effort to solve the jig-saw puzzle by manipulating pieces of evidence which have been worn out by constant handling. What I hope will come out of this study is an agreement that the proper solution forces us to reject a general assumption, viz. that all we have to do is to fit the jig-saw pieces together; instead it requires a study of the pieces themselves and for their own sakes, not yet another attempt to fit them together.

When Cuff says that he is not making yet another attempt to fit the jig-saw pieces together, he clearly does not mean that he is not going to try to make sense of all the evidence. He means, as emerges in the course of the article, that he is not going to accept certain overall assumptions about the terms of the problem which have governed previous attempts to make the pieces fit. He is going to look again at the pieces to see if they suggest to him an entirely fresh approach. And this he claims to have found:

A groundwork has been offered for the re-examination of the politics of 56 to 49 B.C. . . . I have hoped to show the impossibility of combining into one coherent whole all the scraps of evidence as to Caesar's position in this period. . . . If the argument presented here is valid these particular problems should take on a different aspect. . . .

52

The evidence on the terminal date cannot be reconciled because there were two views (*at the time*) on what the terminal date was. It is a mistake of method to attempt to make the pieces fit.

Cuff argues, in effect, that the *Lex Vatinia*, authorising Caesar's command in Gaul for five years, was ambiguous: that initially its ambiguity did not matter and was not noticed; but that subsequent legislation brought the ambiguity into the open, yielding two interpretations, one held by Caesar's followers, one by Pompey's. It was for this reason that the jig-saw pieces did not fit.

In this sort of case also it will not do simply to concentrate on finding an agreed starting-point. Of course there will be, and must be, much that historians do in fact agree upon, and it may clarify the position usefully if they first map the area of agreement. But when they reach the controversial points it will become evident that each will have to resist the other's interpretation of the evidence he considers most significant and insist on his own; because, unless it is so interpreted, it will not fit into the overall picture which it seems to him reasonable to draw of the entire episode. Here too, as in the case of critical exegesis, there is a continuous tension between the individual bits of evidence and the overall interpretation, such that (*a*) the overall interpretation has to make sense of the evidence, neither ignoring nor distorting it, (*b*) the evidence has to square with all the other evidence. In extreme cases evidence may be dismissed as untrustworthy — documents as forged, witnesses as biased, etc. — just as in critical exegesis the text may be emended or judged corrupt.

Sometimes the dispute may be settled by the discovery of fresh evidence which gives decisive support to one side. Sometimes a historian of genius offers a solution that puts the whole problem in a new perspective. He appeals to no new evidence, but reintegrates all existing pieces into a more convincing pattern. Then something like the switch in visual gestalt occurs.

It is evident that these examples, taken from critical exegesis

53

and history, have force only in so far as the procedure illustrated is indeed rational and generates conclusions which are capable of being true or false. Their usefulness in the present context may be challenged on both counts.

(i) *Rationality*. Some would argue that history, in contrast with science, is irredeemably subjective. This view is associated with Karl Popper. J. A. Passmore summarises it as follows [13]:

> Popper's criticism amounts to this: the hypotheses of history are *ad hoc* hypotheses, and we are free to choose as we like between *ad hoc* hypotheses. In contrast the hypotheses of science are designed to apply to situations other than those which suggested them; in this way the facts compel us to choose between them. We accept the hypothesis which leads us to expect, as other hypotheses do not, certain changes to take place which we then observe to occur. In history, however, all the relevant facts are already before us. Thus in choosing between hypotheses, the historian is not, as the physicist is, *constrained* by the facts, and in this difference the subjectivity of history resides.

In replying to this criticism, Passmore usefully develops the analogy with the interpretation of a text — in this case the work of David Hume [14]:

> Some little time ago, I wrote a book which purported to be an interpretation of Hume's philosophy. One reviewer addressed me somewhat as follows: 'A possible interpretation, but other interpretations are equally possible.' How is one to reply? Obviously this is a case where Popper's difficulty is at its most acute. I can produce as evidence nothing except a passage in Hume's writings; I can do nothing which corresponds to predicting an as yet unobserved colour-shift in Mercury.
>
> Yet at the same time my inquiry, as I conduct it, is not *ad hoc*. Why? Because what happens is something like this: an interpretation is suggested by certain passages in Hume;

54

that interpretation is then confirmed by passages I had not previously so much as noticed, which the proposed interpretation serves to illuminate. Or I discover that passages which I previously could not understand now make good sense.

There is, as Passmore indicates, something akin to experiment in this process of interpretation [15]. He mentions cases where fresh passages serve to confirm his provisional interpretation but, of course, he might find other cases where they tended to refute it, if taken at their face value. The alternatives before him would then be either to abandon his hypothesis and try out another or to see if he could find an interpretation of these seemingly recalcitrant passages which was consistent with it and did not do violence to the text. Scholars do not commonly address themselves explicitly to the philosopher's question: 'In precisely what circumstances would you give up your proposed interpretation entirely?' but they sometimes do give it up — if, for example, the only meaning of a particular word that can be reconciled with it is one which the critic could be persuaded the word did not bear at the time. The final decision would have to be a matter for individual judgement, but a trained and sensitive judgement open to rational persuasion.

Hence a difficulty which has often been noticed in connection with theological reasoning can be seen to arise also in these more straightforward (though not entirely uncontroversial) cases, where it looks very much less intractable. There are circumstances in which the scholar would be prepared to abandon his theory, although it is, in the nature of the case, not possible to specify them accurately in advance. It is not until the complete theory has been constructed that he is, as a rule, able to claim that the evidence to which he has attended at each stage confirms his initial hypothesis beyond all rational doubt, or can decide finally how much weight should be given to a particular passage.

(ii) *Truth or Falsehood.* It is characteristic of the types of argument under discussion that they admit of no clear-cut decision procedure, and there has been a common reluctance to concede that they are capable of leading to conclusions which are true or false. A philosopher who has been particularly sensitive to this question is Wisdom. In his essay, 'Gods', he remarks: 'We can all easily recollect disputes which though they cannot be settled by experiment are yet disputes in which one party may be right and the other wrong and in which both parties may offer reasons and the one better reasons than the other' [16]. Yet he remains characteristically elusive on the question whether disputes of this sort can properly be thought of as concerned with fact. On the one hand he says that such argument 'lends itself to description in terms of conflicting "probabilities". This encourages the feeling that the issue is one of fact — that it is a matter of guessing from the premises at a further fact, at what is to come. But this is a muddle' [17]. On the other hand he remarks later [18] that

> If we say as we did at the beginning that when a difference as to the existence of a God is not one as to future happenings then it is not experimental and therefore not as to the facts, we must not forthwith assume that there is no right and wrong about it, no rationality or irrationality, no appropriateness or inappropriateness, no procedure which tends to settle it, *nor even that this procedure is in no sense a discovery of new facts.*

And then, tantalisingly, 'After all, even in science, this is not so'.

It is hard to see why there should be these doubts in the sort of case we have been considering. It is, surely, a question of fact whether in a certain passage Plato or Hume meant this or that and whether Marvell is being ironical in his treatment of Irish attitudes to Cromwell; also whether the conflict of opinion among our sources about the terminal date of Caesar's command in Gaul was or was not due to an ambiguity in the text of the *Lex Vatinia* [19]. Similarly it is a question of fact whether X did or did not commit the murder, whether Y did or did not paint the picture. If

56

members of the jury differ about the former question or art historians about the latter, it must be the case that at least one party is mistaken. There would, therefore, seem to be cases in which an argument which does not purport to be a proof or to rely on strict probability is capable of providing reasonable grounds for a conclusion about a matter of fact.

Thus far, no more than a *prima facie* case has been made for holding that theological argument resembles such arguments in whatever are the relevant respects. It certainly looks as if the different considerations to which the Christian apologist appeals do reinforce one another in somewhat the same fashion as is exemplified in the kind of historical and critical disputes we have been reviewing.

But it is open to a critic to object that there are important differences between the theological case and these others which make it impossible to sustain the required analogy. Some of these objections will be considered in the next chapter.

4 A Strategy for the Defence of the Rationality of Theism

The point of the comparison between such procedures as those of history and critical exegesis and those of theology was to suggest that theology is not alone in relying on arguments which have force but cannot be regarded as demonstrations or as based on strict probabilities. If there are such cumulative arguments, theological reasoning would certainly seem to make use of them. Thus I. M. Crombie, in his paper 'Theology and Falsification', discusses what he calls 'theistic interpretations of our experience' [1].

Those who so interpret need not be so inexpert in logic as to suppose that there is anything of the nature of a deductive or inductive argument which leads from a premiss asserting the existence of the area of experience in question to a conclusion expressing belief in God. . . . All that is necessary is that he [the theist] should be honestly convinced that, in interpreting them [his experiences], as he does, theistically, he is in some sense facing them more honestly, bringing out more of what they contain or involve than could be done by interpreting them in any other way. The one interpretation is preferred to the other, not because the latter is thought to be refutable on paper, but because it is judged to be unconvincing in the light of familiarity with the facts. There is a partial parallel to this in historical judgment. Where you and I differ in our interpretation of a series of events, there is nothing outside the events in question which can over-rule either of us, so that each man must accept the interpretation which seems, on fair and critical scrutiny, the most convincing to him.

The strategy of this sort of defence of the rationality of theism would seem to be as follows. First of all what Crombie calls 'theistic interpretation' is seen as a special case of metaphysical reasoning. That is to say, it attempts to provide an account of everything there is in accordance with intelligible principles which are not identical with those employed in empirical inquiry. The standard objection to metaphysical systems [2], that there are no rules in accordance with which they can be submitted to the test of observation, is met, or at least mitigated, by the claim that there are other types of interpretation of more limited scope which cannot be confirmed or falsified by experiment, yet which may be supported by good or bad reasons and judged true or false accordingly.

Critics of this defence are likely to raise two major objections:

(i) They may argue that there is a fundamental difference between metaphysical systems or world-views, which claim in principle to accommodate all possible experience, and other more circumscribed pieces of explanation or interpretation of a kind illustrated by the historical and exegetical examples. And this is, indeed, recognised by Crombie. The parallel, he says, is only partial because 'in historical (and literary) interpretation there is something which to some extent controls one's interpretation, and that is one's general knowledge of human nature; and in metaphysical interpretation there is nothing analogous to this' [3]. Similarly, it might be said, the literary critic, even before he starts his exegesis, has ample reason to believe that the text had an author (or authors) and there is, therefore, a presumption (although a defeasible one) that the whole thing makes some kind of sense. There is no similar presumption that the universe as a whole makes sense or has an author. As we saw, the parable of the Explorers fails in the same respect. It is reasonable to suppose that the first man when he fancies he notices something odd about the holes is unconsciously comparing them with holes which he has previously encountered and which contained posts. But there is no analogy to this in the religious case. Nobody is in a position to

60

compare putative religious experiences with others which are known to be experiences of God.

(ii) They may draw attention to the fact that the examples of historical and critical reasoning which are said to be analogous to metaphysical reasoning are of a comparatively straightforward and non-controversial kind. The Roman historians who disagree with one another about the problem of the termination of Caesar's command in Gaul agree entirely as to the sort of solution which would be acceptable and as to the concepts involved in the scholarly treatment of the question. Similarly the two scholars disputing over the interpretation of a text share assumptions as to the sort of meaning it is likely to have. In neither case is there in practice much difficulty in distinguishing between interpretations which are respectable academic exercises (although in particular cases they may be rejected as implausible) and crack-brained interpretations which the editor of a scholarly journal would dismiss as unworthy of serious consideration. It is only within the recognised limits of historical study or critical discussion that the sort of argument in question has any claim to be regarded as rational. Therefore, whatever may be the correct analysis of arguments of this sort, and even if they do not conform to the normal pattern of deductive or inductive reasoning, they give little or no support to the claims that are made for the rationality of large-scale metaphysical systems. This, it might be said, becomes immediately obvious if we suppose a historical or exegetical argument in which religious or other metaphysical presuppositions are involved. The question whether there is a historical basis for the miracle narratives of the New Testament would be a case in point. Whether or not it is in principle possible to decide on any rational ground whether a miracle took place, the difference between the disputants in such a case may be of a kind that is not resolvable by ordinary historical methods. There may be a fundamental disagreement between the parties as to whether a miracle can happen, so that a cumulative argument of the sort involved in the dispute about Caesar's command in Gaul cannot even begin to get under way. There is a similar

61

difference between the question whether an epistle was written by St Paul and the question whether it was written under divine inspiration.

It is not only the presence or absence of religious presuppositions that may remove a disagreement from the non-controversial realm within which alone, so it might be said, it remains capable of being resolved by argument. The difference between the presuppositions of a liberal and a Marxist historian may be radical enough to have this effect, and so may that between a Freudian and a non-Freudian literary critic. In these cases too the dispute may be of a kind in which neither party is prepared to countenance the possibility in principle of the sort of solution towards which the other is working.

If, then, the strategy I have outlined is to have any hope of success, examples must be found of disputes in which the participants put forward non-demonstrative, non-inductive arguments of a cumulative kind, involving more or less profound conceptual differences, but which are nevertheless capable of rational solution. And if this requirement can be met, there will remain the difficulty about the unrestricted scope of metaphysical systems, to which examples of less ambitious schemes of interpretation can afford no analogy [4].

The critic of the proposed strategy suspects that putative examples will always turn out, when carefully examined, to fall into one or other of two classes. Either they are capable of rational solution, but involve no profound conceptual differences; or they involve profound conceptual differences, but are not capable of rational solution. In neither case do they give any support to the thesis that a rational case can be made for a system of religious belief.

It is characteristic of disputes involving profound conceptual differences that the disputants can always accommodate any evidence or arguments put forward by their opponents, which each interprets and assesses in terms of his own fundamental principles. The competing systems of thought are so ramified that it is difficult, if not impossible to state the issues involved in ways that do not beg the question in favour of one side or the other. Hence the parties tend to 'talk through one another' and to be lost in mutual incomprehension.

That this is true of the debate between theists and atheists is a matter of common experience. Here, for instance, is Crombie endeavouring to explain to an uncommitted reader his understanding of the fundamental theistic conviction that the world is contingent [5]:

> Let me say something about the sense of contingency, the conviction which people have, it may be in blinding moments, or it may be in a permanent disposition of a man's mind, that we, and the whole world in which we live, derive our being from something outside us. The first thing that I want to say is that such a conviction is to no extent like the conclusion of an argument; the sense of dependence feels not at all like being persuaded by arguments, but like seeing, seeing, as it were, through a gap in the rolling mists of argument, which alone, one feels, could conceal the obvious truth. One is not *persuaded* to believe that one is contingent; rather one feels that it is only by persuasion that one could ever believe anything else.

Here, by contrast, is a sympathetic critic, Ronald Hepburn, struggling to understand what is meant by such explanations of the cosmological argument [6]:

> What is hardest of all to decide . . . is whether or not there *is* such a relation as the sophisticated versions of the Cosmological Argument speak of, or how we could decide whether there is or not. Are they gesturing towards, stammering about, some real but scarcely expressible relation, or are they creating the illusion of one only? . . . We may simply reach an impasse in which the objector says, 'Well, there's no room left for any relation at all'; and the defender says, 'If you can't see it, you can't see it.' But, to me, all these analogies point to a relation that is mysterious but real.

63

A less sympathetic critic, Flew, is prepared to dismiss the argument as either logically vicious or 'nothing but a bit of wishfulness chastely parading in a muddle about explanation' [7].

It seems reasonable to assume that Crombie's difficulty in explaining what he has in mind is due in part to the constraint imposed upon him by the attempt to describe one element only in a total Christian theistic system and to do so in a religiously neutral vocabulary. Hepburn's difficulty in grasping what is intended by 'the sophisticated versions of the Cosmological Argument' is similarly traceable in part to its isolation from the rest of the theistic scheme. Flew is saved the trouble of trying to understand it by his antecedent confidence that it involves assumptions which, in terms of his own world-view, cannot make sense.

It has already been suggested that this sort of situation is not peculiar to disputes between theists and atheists. A parallel which may prove illuminating is provided by the fundamental shifts of vision that occur in science, as illustrated in T. S. Kuhn's 'The Structure of Scientific Revolutions' [8]. Kuhn gives a number of examples, the most familiar, and the most readily intelligible to the non-scientist, being the switch from Aristotle's to Galileo's theory of motion [9] :

> Since remotest antiquity most people have seen one or another heavy body swinging back and forth on a string or chain until it finally comes to rest. To the Aristotelians, who believed that a heavy body is moved by its own nature from a higher position to a state of natural rest at a lower one, the swinging body was simply falling with difficulty. Constrained by a chain, it could achieve rest at its low point only after tortuous motion and a considerable time. Galileo, on the other hand, looking at the swinging body, saw a pendulum, a body that almost succeeded in repeating the same motion over and over again ad infinitum. And having seen that much, Galileo observed other properties of the pendulum as well and constructed many of the most significant and original parts

64

of his new dynamics around them. From the properties of the pendulum, for example, Galileo derived his only full and sound arguments for the independence of weight and rate of fall, as well as for the relationship between vertical height and terminal velocity of motions down inclined planes. All these natural phenomena he saw differently from the way they had been seen before.

Kuhn makes use of an analogy with the now familiar 'switch in visual gestalt' [10]:

What were ducks in the scientist's world before the revolution are rabbits afterwards . . . . Therefore, at times of revolution, when the normal-scientific tradition changes, the scientist's perception of his environment must be re-educated — in some familiar situations he must learn to see a new gestalt. After he has done so the world of his research will seem, here and there, incommensurable with the one he had inhabited before. That is another reason why schools guided by different paradigms are always slightly at cross-purposes.

There is, however, an important difference, Kuhn suggests, between the switch in visual gestalt, and the change in scientific paradigm. In the case of the gestalt demonstration it is appropriate to say that the subject interprets the data differently when he sees a duck or a rabbit. He can learn to direct his attention to the lines on the paper and can come to see these lines without seeing either of the figures. But this is not the case with the change of scientific paradigm. Here the data are not unequivocally stable. 'A pendulum is not a falling stone, nor is oxygen dephlogisticated air. Consequently, the data that scientists collect from these diverse subjects are . . . themselves different' [11]. Hence the process of transition from one paradigm to another is not strictly a change in interpretation, since there are in such a case no fixed data for the scientist to interpret.

This is not to say that a good deal of straightforward interpretation does not occur in science; indeed it comprises most of 'normal science' in which 'the scientist, by virtue of an accepted paradigm, knew what a datum was, what instruments might be used to retrieve it, and what concepts were relevant to its interpretation' [12].

Then Kuhn goes on to make a point which in substance and in language is clearly related to our own concern [13]:

But that interpretive enterprise can only articulate a paradigm, not correct it. Paradigms are not corrigible by normal science at all. Instead, as we have already seen, normal science leads ultimately only to the recognition of anomalies and to crises. And these are terminated, not by deliberation and interpretation, but by a relatively sudden and unstructured event like the gestalt switch. Scientists then often speak of the 'scales falling from their eyes' or of the 'lightning flash' that 'inundates' a previously obscure puzzle, enabling its components to be seen in a new way that for the first time permits its solution. On other occasions the relevant illumination comes in sleep. No ordinary sense of the term 'interpretation' fits these flashes of intuition through which a new paradigm is born. Though such intuitions depend upon the experience, both anomalous and congruent, gained with the old paradigm, they are not logically or piecemeal linked to particular items of that experience as an interpretation would be. Instead, they gather up large portions of that experience and transform them to a rather different bundle of experience that will thereafter be linked piecemeal to the new paradigm but not to the old.

Kuhn's language here is reminiscent of Ian Ramsey with his talk of 'disclosures', and his metaphors of 'bells ringing, light dawning, ice breaking, etc.' Ramsey, I think, is best taken as drawing attention to the importance of some such 'paradigm shift' in the religious case. When a man is converted (whether this process is dramatically sudden or not), he begins to 'see everything in a fresh light'. This is not to be thought of as his having simply (or even at all) some specific 'inner experience', but as his coming to organise his entire 'world' in a different way.

I introduced Kuhn's treatment of scientific revolutions into the discussion as providing a parallel to the mutual incomprehension that there often is between those who see the world as requiring an explanation of some kind and those who are clear that there is (or even can be) no such requirement. The former speak of 'intellectual pressures' which the latter dismiss as purely psychological. What we are confronted with here is a clash between two incompatible metaphysical systems, each of which claims to give an adequate (but not, of course, complete) account of everything there is, and to anatomise the kinds of explanation that are legitimate. As has often been pointed out, this has the consequence that it is not possible to judge between them by criteria all of which are entirely neutral. The question is, however, whether it follows that it is not possible to judge between them at all.

To some the answer to this question may seem obvious. For is it not almost a commonplace of philosophical discussion that it is not possible to judge between them? Consider, for example, G. J. Warnock [14]:

Much admirable philosophical work has been done upon the notion of 'ways of seeing', of angles of vision, of — to speak more ponderously — alternative conceptual systems. We have become familiar enough with the idea that phenomena may be viewed in more than one way, comprehended within more than one theory, interpreted by more than one set of explanatory concepts. It has thus become almost impossible to believe that some *one* way of seeing, some *one* sort of theory, has an exclusive claim to be the *right* way; the notion of 'reality' itself, it would commonly be held, must be given its sense in terms of some particular theory or view, so that the claim that any such theory reveals or corresponds to 'reality' can be given a circular justification which is also open, in just the same way, to quite other views as well.

If, as Kuhn's thesis appears to suggest, a similar phenomenon appears also in science at times of paradigm shift, we may be less inclined than Warnock is to acquiesce in this sort of conceptual relativism. It is worth looking again at

Kuhn, therefore, to see how he deals with the problems raised by the need to choose between paradigms. He claims, first of all, that orthodox verification theories do not meet the case because they rely on the notion of pure or neutral observation languages. Since, from his own standpoint, no such language is possible, and observations have to be described in terms that are dependent on a particular paradigm, it follows that the process of testing cannot enable the scientist to choose between such paradigms. Although this argument, if valid, would seem to hold also against Popper's falsification theory, Kuhn relies in his criticism of Popper on another argument which does not depend on the rejection of observation-languages [15]:

As I have repeatedly emphasised before, no theory ever solves all the puzzles with which it is confronted at a given time; nor are the solutions already achieved often perfect. On the contrary, it is just the incompleteness and imperfection of the existing data-theory fit that, at any time, define many of the puzzles that characterize normal science. If any and every failure to fit were ground for theory rejection, all theories ought to be rejected at all times. On the other hand, if only severe failure to fit justifies theory rejection, then Popperians will require some criterion of 'improbability' or 'degree of falsification'. In developing one they will almost certainly encounter the same network of difficulties that has haunted the advocates of the various probabilistic verification theories.

Then he goes on:

To the historian, at least, it makes little sense to suggest that verification is establishing the agreement of fact with theory. All historically significant theories have agreed with the facts, but only more or less. There is no more precise answer to the question whether or how well an individual theory fits the facts. But ... it makes a good deal of sense to ask which of two actual and competing theories fits the facts *better*.

68

But this, he immediately confesses, oversimplifies [16]:

> This formulation, however, makes the task of choosing between pradigms look both easier and more familiar than it is. If there were but one set of scientific problems, one world within which to work on them, and one set of standards for their solution, paradigm competition might be settled more or less routinely by some process like counting the number of problems solved by each. But, in fact, these conditions are never met completely. The proponents of competing paradigms are always at least slightly at cross-purposes. Neither side will grant all the non-empirical assumptions that the other needs in order to make its case . . . they are bound partly to talk through each other. Though each may hope to convert the other to his way of seeing his science and its problems, neither may hope to prove his case. The competition between paradigms is not the sort of battle that can be resolved by proofs.

My motive in introducing this discussion of Kuhn's thesis will now be clear. If Kuhn is right, the phenomenon of paradigm shift as he describes it in science does indeed bear a strong analogy to the situation which we have already discerned in the controversy between the theist and the atheist. The resemblances may be summed up as follows:

1. Kuhn remarks that 'schools guided by different paradigms are always slightly at cross-purposes . . . . They are bound to talk through each other . . . the proponents of competing paradigms will often disagree about the list of problems that any candidate for paradigm must solve.' This reminds one strikingly of the situation in which theists and atheists do not agree either as to what are the problems to be solved, or as to the characterisation of the 'facts' or the 'evidence'. The theist believes that the questions 'Why is there anything at all?' and 'Why does the universe have the sort of order that it does?' state problems which require a solution. The atheist denies that they are problems at all. Hence the theist's claim to solve these problems carries no weight with him. Nor are they both able to accept, for

example, an agreed, purely phenomenological description of what are claimed as 'religious experiences'.

2. When a paradigm shift occurs, a comparatively large-scale transformation of the individual's 'world' takes place. Kuhn writes [17]

> To make the transition to Einstein's universe, the whole conceptual web˜ whose strands are space, time, matter, force, and so on, had to be shifted and laid down again on nature whole. Only men who had together undergone or failed to undergo that transformation would be able to discover precisely what they agreed or disagreed about. Communication across the revolutionary divide is inevitably partial.

The parallel with religious conversion is too obvious to require elaboration. Hence:

3. As we have already noticed, the language which scientists use to describe the experience of undergoing a paradigm shift is strongly reminiscent of the language of religious conversion. The scientist will talk of 'the scales falling from his eyes', etc. Indeed, Kuhn himself uses the word 'conversion' [18]:

> ... before they can hope to communicate fully, one group or the other must experience the conversion that we have been calling a paradigm shift. Just because it is a transition between incommensurables, the transition between competing paradigms cannot be made a step at a time, forced by logic and neutral experience. Like the gestalt switch, it must occur all at once (though not necessarily in an instant) or not at all.

It will be necessary at a later stage to consider what conclusions should be drawn from the degree of resemblance that appears to exist between the problem of deciding between scientific paradigms and the problem of choosing between competing metaphysical systems. Before proceeding

70

to this task it is worthwhile investigating another comparison, this time with philosophy itself.

It may seem odd to introduce philosophy as an example in this discussion, since we are looking for parallels to what happens when different metaphysical schemes are in conflict, and metaphysics is not simply analogous to philosophy; it is itself a branch of philosophy. It is, however, still in some quarters a somewhat suspect branch. Warnock in the work quoted earlier is at pains to distinguish philosophy from matters of *Weltanschauung*, and the approval now increasingly given to metaphysics is still a somewhat qualified approval. If it should appear that philosophy of an entirely respectable kind shares the peculiar features which have brought metaphysics into disrepute, this would have some force against those who can see no basis for choosing between alternative metaphysical schemes.

And it certainly does look as if the phenomenon of paradigm shift is endemic in philosophy, as is recognised by F. Waismann in 'How I See Philosophy' [19]:

Arguments are used in such a discussion, not as proofs, though, but rather as means to make him see things he had not noticed before: e.g. to dispel wrong analogies, to stress similarities with other cases and in this way to bring about something like a shift in perspective. However, there is no way of proving him wrong or bullying him into mental acceptance of the proposal: when all is said and done the decision is his.

A great deal of philosophical argument is concerned with the drawing of conclusions from premisses in a straightforwardly deductive way, but this cannot be the whole of it, since the philosopher has to satisfy himself as to the comparative merits of rival theories all of which are internally consistent. In order to do this he must evaluate their consequences; that is to say, he must decide whether they yield conclusions which are true or false, intelligible or unintelligible when applied to the relevant subject-matter. It is, characteristically, the arguments deployed at this stage about which Waismann

71

is justified in remarking that 'philosophic arguments are not deductive; therefore they are not rigorous; and therefore they don't prove anything. Yet they have force' [20]. The sort of problem involved is well illustrated by Ayer [21]:

There must always be some method of approach. The value of the method can be tested only by its results. Here, however, there is the difficulty that the results themselves must be evaluated. If they are tested by the same criteria as are used in obtaining them, they are bound to be favourable so long as the method is consistent. But then this whole proceeding lies open to the charge of begging the question. On the other hand, it is not to be expected that one should employ any other criteria than those which from the outset have been assumed to be correct. Thus, so long as it is free from inner contradiction, it is hard to see how any philosophical thesis can be refuted; and equally hard to see how it can ever be proved.

The point that Ayer is making here seems to be identical with that made by Warnock in discussing world-views. Warnock, as we saw, takes this to show that no view has any exclusive claim to be the right one. Ayer does not, I think, draw this conclusion. He illustrates the contention he has just made by reference to physicalism [22]:

Let us take for example the thesis of physicalism; that all statements which ostensibly refer to mental states or processes are translatable into statements about physical occurrences. The obvious way to refute it is to produce a counter-example, which in this case seems quite easy. There are any number of statements about people's thoughts and sensations and feelings which appear to be logically independent of any statement about their bodily condition or behaviour. But the adherent to physicalism may not recognize these examples: he may insist that they be interpreted in accordance with his principles. He will do so not because this is the meaning that they manifestly have, but because he has convinced himself on *a priori*

72

grounds that no other way of interpreting them is possible. Our only hope then is to make the interpretations appear so strained that the assumptions on which they rest become discredited. As for the proof of any such thesis, it rests on the absence of any refutation of this sort. So long as we cannot find any convincing counter-example, the thesis is allowed to stand. In this respect the procedure followed in philosophy is like that of the natural sciences.

Ayer says that a philosophical thesis is allowed to stand so long as we cannot find, not just a counter-example, but a 'convincing counter-example' which the thesis under attack is able to accommodate only with considerable strain. A philosophical thesis, when confronted with such counter-examples, is likely to undergo modification, with a view to finding a version of the thesis which will at the same time cope better with the counter-examples and maintain what was attractive in the original formulation. And when two philosophical theses are being compared, the choice between them will have to depend, not simply on whether counter-examples can be found to either, but on how convincing each is when it has done its best to accommodate all the relevant facts (including, of course, how plausible is its determination of what is relevant and what is fact).

The way in which Ayer proceeds to tackle the problem presented by this typical situation in philosophy bears a striking resemblance to Kuhn's treatment of paradigm choice in science, and at the same time answers, by implication, the most serious objection against the use of philosophy as an example, alongside natural science, in this connection. The objection is that philosophy, unlike natural science, does not pronounce upon matters of fact; in Wittgenstein's phrase 'it leaves everything as it is'. Ayer answers it by questioning the assumption that 'it is possible to supply a neutral record of facts which is free from any taint of theory; a common bedrock for divergent interpretations' [23]. Thus it is of doubtful truth to say that Berkeley and the naïve realist do not disagree about any matter of fact — they both accept the same observable states of affairs. 'But what are these

73

observable states of affairs? The Berkeleian describes them in a way that the naive realist finds unintelligible: the naïve realist describes them in a way that the Berkeleian might regard as begging the question against him' [24]. If it is true that fact and interpretation cannot be wholly divorced,

> If this is right, it appears that philosophy does after all intrude upon questions of empirical fact. Once it is established what is to count as fact, that is, once the criteria are settled, it is an empirical and not a philosophical question whether they are satisfied. *But adoption of these criteria implies the acceptance of a given conceptual system, and the appraisal of conceptual systems does fall within the province of philosophy* (my italics) [25].

If this conclusion is correct, it takes with it, I suggest, any hope of making a neat distinction between (respectable) philosophical analysis and (disreputable) metaphysics. For 'the appraisal of conceptual systems' is not a bad description of what has normally been called metaphysics.

The purpose of introducing these discussions of natural science and philosophy was to meet the objection that the earlier examples drawn from critical exegesis and history failed at a crucial point in that they provided no parallel to the most problematic feature of the dispute between theists and atheists: that it is a dispute, as they are not, in which fundamental conceptual differences are involved. It was therefore necessary to offer examples of disputes which possess this further feature, but which are nevertheless capable, at least in principle, of being resolved by rational means. However, the critic of this entire strategy may well not be satisfied with these examples. The trouble with them, he may complain, is not only that the analogy with the debate about theism is not close enough, but also that, however close the analogy, the examples themselves are far too ambiguous to give the argument the support it needs. For both Kuhn's account of paradigm choice in science and Ayer's account of philosophical argument raise serious doubts as to whether either can count as a rational activity.

74

5 Rational Choice between Scientific Paradigms

Our discussion up to this point of the rationality of religious belief has proved inconclusive because the analogies we have claimed to discern between religious systems of thought and other systems have turned out to be themselves ambiguous. The analogies were intended to suggest that the same sort of disagreement as occurs between theists and atheists is also found between proponents of rival scientific paradigms and rival philosophical theories. But the analogies are open to attack on two grounds. The first is that, even if the analogies hold in other relevant respects, they do not give any support to the claim that the disagreement between theists and atheists is capable of rational solution. For there is a precisely similar doubt as to whether a rational choice can be made between scientific paradigms and philosophical theories. The second is that in any case the analogies do not hold in all the relevant respects. There are peculiarities of the religious case which should prevent us assimilating it to the others.

Meanwhile the resemblance between the problems faced by philosophers of religion on the one hand and philosophers of science on the other is striking enough to make it worth exploring further the possibility that one set of problems may throw light on the other. In each case it is tempting to argue, on the lines of chapter 3, that although the disputes which arise cannot be settled by appeal to strict proof or inductive probabilities, nevertheless it is in principle possible for one side or the other to be rationally preferred because it makes better sense of all the available evidence. And in each case it may be objected to this argument that it is only within certain 'basic presuppositions' or 'categorial frames' or 'conceptual schemes' that differences can be resolved in the informal ways suggested; when, however, what is in question is a choice between these, there can be no rational way of making it, because the 'basic presuppositions', etc., determine for each system what is to count as 'a fact' or as 'evidence' and what are to be the criteria of rational assessment. Hence one cannot without begging the question argue that one conceptual scheme 'makes better overall sense' than another or 'fits the facts better' or is more 'satisfactory' or 'plausible'.

This basic position underlies a number of alternative accounts of the disagreement between theists and atheists, such as the following:

(i) That the criteria of the meaning and truth of religious statements are to be found wholly within religion itself. This is the position which Nielsen calls 'Wittgensteinian Fideism', and which has been extensively developed by D. Z. Phillips [1].

(ii) That different world-views take their origin from different 'absolute presuppositions' (R. G. Collingwood [2]) or 'bliks' (R. M. Hare [3]) or 'basic commitments' (R. B. Braithwaite [4]), which are not themselves open to rational criticism.

(iii) That the religious believer operates within 'the circle of faith' (John Hick [5]) or from the standpoint of a 'confessional theology' (H. R. Niebuhr [6]). Those who adopt this basic position in relation to religious belief usually (but not always) put it forward as a quite general thesis of which religious belief is, simply, a special case, and which can be illustrated also in a range of non-religious cases. The best way to proceed, therefore, would seem to be to consider first some of the non-religious cases. If the non-religious disputes appear to be incapable of rational solution, it seems likely *a fortiori* that the same will be true of the debate between theists and atheists. If, on the other hand, such disputes turn out to be, in principle, amenable to rational solution, it will then be appropriate to go on and inquire whether there are additional features of the religious dispute which make it remain intractable, while the others are not. The non-religious case which has been most thoroughly investigated is the scientific one, to which I therefore return.

Kuhn's thesis, as has been seen in Chapter 4, is twofold:

(i) It is not possible to decide between competing scientific 'paradigms' by appeal to the facts because what constitutes a fact is determined by the relevant paradigm.

(ii) The 'evaluative procedures' characteristic of 'normal science' cannot be employed in making a decision between paradigms because 'these depend in part on a particular paradigm and that paradigm is at issue'.

Decisions between paradigms are, however, made and Kuhn claims that in the end only a sociological account, not a logical one, can be given of the way such decisions are arrived at [7]:

> ... confronted with the problem of theory-choice, the structure of my response runs roughly as follows: take a *group* of the ablest available people with the most appropriate motivation; train them in some science and in the specialties relevant to the choice at hand; imbue them with the value system, the ideology, current in their discipline (and to a great extent in other scientific fields as well); and, finally, *let them make the choice*. If that technique does not account for scientific development as we know it, then no other will. There can be no set of rules of choice adequate to dictate desired *individual* behaviour in the concrete cases that scientists will meet in the course of their careers. Whatever scientific progress may be, we must account for it by examining the nature of the scientific group, discovering what it values, what it tolerates, and what it disdains.

(i) The first part of Kuhn's argument, which impugns the neutrality of facts, is directed against what Imre Lakatos calls 'naïve falsificationism'; the doctrine that science proceeds straightforwardly by subjecting hypotheses to the arbitrament of fact and abandoning those that fail the test. Against this position it is legitimate to object that the scientist often has to choose between two high level theories and that what is to count as a fact may in such cases depend on the choice of a theory. How this occurs is made clear by Lakatos in his discussion of Kuhn's thesis. He agrees in effect with Kuhn that more than one theory is normally in question, i.e., that what is required is a 'pluralistic' model; and in terms of this model shows how the dependence of 'facts' upon theory may come about [8]:

> In the pluralistic model the clash is not 'between theories and facts', but between two high-level theories: between an *interpretative theory* to provide the facts and an *explanatory theory* to explain them; and the interpretative theory may be on quite as high a level as the explanatory theory . . . . The problem is how to repair an *inconsistency* between the 'explanatory theory' under test and the — explicit or hidden — 'interpretative' theories; or, if you wish, *the problem is which theory to consider as the 'interpretative' one which provides the 'hard' facts and which the 'explanatory' one which 'tentatively' explains* them.

Thus a decision has to be made, and this decision cannot be determined by those 'facts' whose recognition as facts depends on the choice as to which theory is the interpretative one. In other words, when a scientist is looking for a theory to explain certain facts, the facts which he is seeking to explain can themselves generally be regarded as theories in relation to other facts, and it is always in principle possible, and sometimes in scientific practice desirable, to call them in question.

Lakatos gives an example. If a big radio-star is discovered with a system of satellites orbiting it, scientists may wish to test some gravitational theory on it. Jodrell Bank provides, let us suppose, observations yielding space-time co-ordinates of the planets, and these are inconsistent with the theory. The scientists carrying out the research would normally accept the observations as falsifying the gravitational theory. But, as Lakatos puts it, 'these basic statements are not 'observational' in the usual sense, only ' "observational" '. They are arrived at by an experimental technique based on the well-corroborated theory of radio optics. Radio optics is used uncritically, as background knowledge, but 'If our best gravitational theory is refuted by the experimental tech-

78

niques of Jodrell Bank, why not interpret the result as the overthrow of radio optics?' [9]. In that case the gravitational theory would be regarded as providing the facts and the theory of radio optics as being falsified by them [10].

But, although in such a case some of the facts are 'paradigm-relative', there are others, and they are the overwhelming majority, which are not in dispute between the two theories. It would clearly, for instance, be possible to describe the operations carried out by Jodrell Bank and the experimental findings in language which would be entirely neutral as between the theories in question. Indeed, that there are such 'neutral' facts is a precondition of the scientific enterprise; they are what ultimately science has to explain. The point has been well made by D. D. Evans [11]:

> It is ... true that the observations [of scientists] are usually reported in a language which includes scientific terms that are relatively theoretical or interpretive as compared with the everyday language of common-sense. But the scientific terms are linked to common-sense terms though they are not reducible to common-sense terms. If a non-scientist in a laboratory sees no spark or feels no tingling pain on touching a wire, the scientist's report concerning an electrical discharge may be undermined or even falsified.

The claim, then, that proponents of different scientific paradigms do not agree as to what constitute 'the facts' is true only up to a point. The facts which may be at issue in this way are those whose specification depends on the acceptance of a theory which is taken to be interpretative in the manner described by Lakatos. Whether, for example, in Lakatos's illustration it is the gravitational theory or the theory of radio optics which is to be taken as providing 'the hard facts' is a matter for decision. But this decision is made within a framework of agreed facts which are not at issue and these include (a) a very large range of facts specified in terms of scientific theories which the proponents of both paradigms accept, (*b*) common-sense facts of the sort that are not in dispute at all between scientists, agreement as to which is presupposed in all scientific activity.

Indeed, if this were not the case, not only would rival scientific theories not be testable, but they would not be rival theories at all; for their rivalry consists in their purporting to offer alternative explanations of the same facts [12].

(ii) The second part of Kuhn's argument maintains that the proponents of different paradigms must disagree as to the criteria by which the evidence is assessed:

> Like the choice between competing political institutions, that between competing paradigms proves to be a choice between incompatible modes of community life. Because it has that character, the choice is not and cannot be determined merely by the evaluative procedures characteristic of normal science, for these depend in part upon a particular paradigm, and that paradigm is at issue. When paradigms enter, as they must, into a debate about paradigm choice, their role is necessarily circular. Each group uses its own paradigm to argue in that paradigm's defence [13].

It seems, however, that Kuhn intends a very strict interpretation of criteria or 'evaluative procedures' for the purpose of this argument. It is not necessary to investigate here precisely what he has in mind, since he does freely allow that there are good reasons for choosing one theory rather than another of a kind that are not conditional upon acceptance of a particular paradigm. He recognises that such considerations as accuracy, scope, simplicity and fruitfulness are relevant and that they transcend particular paradigms. Indeed his disagreement with Lakatos does not appear to consist in his differing from him as to the sort of decisions involved in choice between paradigms; it is, rather, a second order disagreement as to whether such decisions are properly to be regarded as rational, or whether they are, as he puts it, 'irreducibly sociological'. Thus, taking up Lakatos's discussion and employing his vocabulary, Kuhn writes [14]:

Scientists must, for example, *decide* which statements to make 'unfalsifiable by *fiat*' and which not. Or, dealing with a probabilistic theory, they must *decide* on a probability threshold below which statistical evidence will be held 'inconsistent' with that theory. Above all, viewing theories as research programmes to be evaluated over time, scientists must *decide* whether a given programme at a given time is 'progressive' (whence scientific) or 'degenerative' (whence pseudo-scientific). If the first, it is to be pursued; if the latter, rejected.

What, then, determines for Kuhn whether these decisions are arrived at rationally or whether they are such that ultimately only a sociological account can be given of them? The answer would seem to be that Kuhn will regard them as rational if and only if Lakatos can specify rules for discriminating, e.g., between progressive and degenerative problem-shifts, 'rules which would dictate their outcomes' [15]. Such rules he distinguishes from judgements of value [16]:

What I am denying then is neither the existence of good reasons nor that these reasons are of the sort usually described. I am, however, insisting that such reasons constitute values to be used in making choices rather than rules of choice . . . . Simplicity, scope, fruitfulness and even accuracy can be judged quite differently (which is not to say that they may be judged arbitrarily) by different people. Again, they may differ in their conclusions without violating any accepted rule.

In this passage and in others like it Kuhn firmly rejects the charge that he is espousing irrationalism. And indeed the procedure he is describing as typical of scientists in choosing one theory rather than another is identical with that which I have taken to be characteristic of reasoning in the humanities. With respect to philosophy Kuhn makes the point himself. He lists as good reasons for theory choice 'reasons of exactly the kind standard in philosophy of science:

81

accuracy, scope, simplicity, fruitfulness, and the like' [17].

This being so, it looks very much as if Lakatos and Kuhn agree as to the sort of procedures actually involved in theory choice; and it is hard to see why they should not also agree that they are rational procedures. Lakatos asserts that 'in Kuhn's view there can be no logic, but only psychology of discovery' [18], and it is, perhaps, the acceptance by both parties of this sharp dichotomy that is responsible for their misunderstanding. It seems to be assumed on both sides that unless it is possible to specify rules for the making of choices, unless, that is, the making of choices is strictly a matter of logic, it can only be material for the psychology of scientists or the sociology of science. The oddness of this assumption emerges clearly if one applies it to the case of philosophy. Kuhn rightly points out that one of the most interesting features of the debate between himself and his critics, as it is conducted in the pages of 'Criticism and the Growth of Knowledge', is that it itself exemplifies the type of disagreement to the correct analysis of which it is devoted [19]:

> One especially interesting aspect of this volume is, then, that it provides a developed example of a minor culture clash, of the severe communication difficulties which characterize such clashes, and of the linguistic techniques deployed in an attempt to end them. Read as an example, it could be an object for study and analysis, providing concrete information concerning a type of developmental episode about which we know very little. For some readers, I suspect, the recurrent failure of these essays to intersect on intellectual issues will provide this book's greatest interest.

The debate in question is a philosophical one and Kuhn's comment recalls the claim advanced in Chapter 4 of the present book that philosophy affords examples of disagreements which cannot be settled by demonstrative arguments or appeal to strict probabilities, yet are in principle capable of being settled rationally. Such disagreements can and often do involve more or less far-reaching conceptual differences,

82

and it is these which are responsible for that 'failure to intersect on intellectual issues' to which Kuhn draws attention. If Kuhn's hint is followed and we approach the debate between Kuhn and his critics with the question whether it represents an exercise in strict logic or merely material for the psychology of philosophers, it is impossible not to feel that we are being confronted with false alternatives. That it is not the former is lucidly conveyed by Kuhn himself (he is talking about theory-choice) [20]:

In a debate over choice of theory, neither party has access to an argument which resembles a proof in logic or formal mathematics. In the latter, both premises and rules of inference are stipulated in advance. If there is disagreement about conclusions, the parties to the debate can retrace their steps one by one, checking each against prior stipulation. At the end of the process, one or other must concede that at an isolable point in the argument he has made a mistake, violated or misapplied a previously accepted rule. After that concession he has no recourse, and his opponent's proof is then compelling. Only if the two discover instead that they differ about the meaning or applicability of a stipulated rule, that their prior agreement does not provide a sufficient basis for proof, does the ensuing debate resemble what inevitably occurs in science.

He then applies this to his argument with Popper:

Nothing about this relatively familiar thesis should suggest that scientists do not *use* logic (and mathematics) in their arguments, including those which aim to persuade a colleague to renounce a favoured theory and embrace another. I am dumbfounded by Sir Karl's attempt to convict me of self-contradiction because I employ logical arguments myself. What might be better said is that I do not expect that, merely because my arguments are logical, they will be compelling. Sir Karl underscores my point, not his, when he describes them as logical but mistaken, and then makes no attempt to isolate the mistake or

83

display its logical character. What he means is that, although my arguments are logical, he disagrees with my conclusion. Our disagreement must be about premises or the manner in which they are to be applied, a situation which is standard among scientists debating theory-choice. When it occurs, their recourse is to persuasion as a prelude to the possibility of proof.

In all this Kuhn seems to me to be clearly right. But it does not follow that only a psychological or a sociological account can be given of the sort of reasoning involved. If this were indeed the case it would not be reasoning at all, and Kuhn's critics would be justified in charging him with irrationalism.

If this analysis of the situation is correct, it would seem that in this case the 'minor culture clash' occurs in the context of a major presupposition which is accepted by both parties to the debate: that a choice between theories (whether scientific or philosophical) is rational if and only if it is possible to specify in advance rules acceptable to both parties in accordance with which the choice is to be made. Kuhn is convinced (rightly) that neither in science nor in philosophy are choices of this kind characteristically made. He therefore allows the choices that are characteristically made to be rational only in a Pickwickian sense, of which in the last resort none but a sociological account can be given. Lakatos and Popper (rightly) reject this as irrationalism and in defence of the rationality of science feel compelled to repudiate (unnecessarily) Kuhn's perceptive account of the sort of reasoning that actually occurs.

The motive for introducing this discussion of Kuhn's views on paradigm choice in science was the hope that it might illuminate, by providing an appropriate analogy, two salient features of the debate between theists and atheists. These are:

(i) that it is not amenable to demonstrative argument or appeal to strict probabilities, and

(ii) that it involves more or less fundamental conceptual differences.

In the light of this discussion we may now dismiss the
84

objection that there can be no rational choice between scientific paradigms and that for this reason the comparison is of no assistance to the argument.

It remains to ask whether our conclusions about the possibility of rational choice between scientific paradigms may legitimately be carried over to large-scale metaphysical theories. It has already been noticed that philosophers have been inclined to argue that there can be no possibility of rational choice between world-views or metaphysical systems for the same sort of reasons as tempted Kuhn to similar conclusions about scientific paradigms:

(i) Every metaphysical system prescribes criteria for what, in terms of the system, are to be regarded as 'facts'.

(ii) Every metaphysical system prescribes also what are to be regarded, in terms of the system, as legitimate criteria of assessment.

The problem is well put by W. H. Walsh. He points out that the first requirement in a metaphysical system is that it should cover all the facts (in a way that gives satisfaction to the experts concerned). And then he continues [21]:

Unhappily these tests are more promising in theory than they turn out to be in practice .... Many people reject materialism on the ground that it brusquely dismisses whole areas of experience as illusory, but would a materialist agree that his philosophy left anything out? Suppose it were said that he failed to take account of, say, the phenomena of religious experience or the compelling character of the feeling of moral obligation. His comment would surely be that he not only mentioned these phenomena but explained them, and explained them in the only way which could make them intelligible. In the case of religion, for example, he showed how it was, i.e. in what physical, psychological and perhaps social conditions, people came to have what are commonly called religious experiences and why they were disposed to put a certain construction on those experiences. And if it were suggested to him that this explanation simply omits what is of the essence of the matter, in so far as it says nothing about the cognitive content of such experiences he would reply that it is an illusion to suppose that they have any such content. Having a religious experience is perhaps like being vividly aware of the presence of another person, with the difference that in this case there is no other person to be aware of. The important point, however, is that we can see how the illusion develops and what purpose it serves.

On this he comments:

> The trouble about testing a theory like that of materialism by its capacity to cover all the facts is that there is no general agreement about what 'the facts' are. Facts exist, or perhaps we should say obtain, only from particular points of view, and here points of view are in dispute. The consequence of this is that the metaphysician is necessarily judge in his own case, for though he must admit to an obligation to take account of all the facts as he sees them, it is in the last resort for him to say what is fact and what is not. His office confers on him the duty of giving an overall interpretation, but simultaneously allows him a veto on accepting anything which cannot be fitted into his scheme.

In discussing a very similar example Ayer, as we have seen, makes the entirely sensible suggestion that in such a case our only hope lies in making the interpretation appear so strained that the assumptions upon which it rests become discredited. The trouble with this, however, is that in terms of the account of the nature of metaphysical reasoning that is under discussion it is hard to see how this can be done. For, according to this account, what interpretations are or are not 'strained' will also be determined within one metaphysical system or another.

Walsh himself makes a sustained attempt to deal with the difficulty. He draws attention, as I have done, to the resemblance between metaphysics and literary criticism (i.e.,

86

the interpretation of a text). In both fields, he says, a great writer is 'revelatory' [22]:

He enables us to take a connected view of many different kinds of facts, and in so doing to see them afresh and find in them new significance. And the procedure for authenticating a revelation of this kind is identical in the two spheres: in each case what we have to do is, first, make the interpretative principles clear, and then show that they provide genuine illumination when applied to the detailed facts. Argument can and does come in here, but in the last resort it is a matter of inviting the reader to take the principles and see for himself.

And so he concludes [23]:

We need to recognize plainly that metaphysical principles can no more be fixed in a scientific way than can moral principles. But it does not follow that principles are adopted without reason. We have mentioned already that there are circumstances — failure to cover all the facts or to cover them adequately — in which an honest metaphysician has no choice but to abandon his principles; and whilst it is true that this is more readily recognized in theory than in practice, the pressure of facts is even so felt in this sphere If the reasons to which metaphysicians appeal do not, as they themselves suppose, necessitate, they nevertheless incline. Despite the appearances, objections to a position formulated in full consciousness of what it amounts to cannot be indefinitely shuffled off.

Walsh then concludes, although with a certain diffidence, that a metaphysical system may be exposed to objections which in the end make it no longer reasonable to continue to accept it. But in the nature of the case it is not possible to specify, except in the very broadest terms, the criteria which are employed in reaching such a decision. It is this fact which, as in the case of the argument about scientific paradigms, tempts philosophers to deny the possibility of

87

rational choice at all. For rational choice to be possible, they are included to insist, there must be some clearly formulable rules for making it, and such rules are not to be found outside the rival systems themselves. The assumption emerges clearly in the following passage by H. A. Hodges [24]:

There are alternative patterns of life and thought, each of which is unintelligible from the standpoint of the others, *and there is no logical road from one to another* [my italics]. There is a road, but it is a road of choice, made as it must be by one who knows that he is moving in the dark, and that nothing less than himself, his future character and life, hangs on the venture. Life is like that, and the choice between fundamentally different attitudes and standpoints is like that. It is unpleasant to those who would like to work it all out as a theorem or to present a clear and distinct solution of the problem; but it is the real predicament of man.

Hodges assumes that unless there is a 'logical road' from the one position to the other, or a 'clear and distinct solution' can be found, there is no possibility of a rational choice; and it is precisely this assumption that we found it necessary to challenge in the debate between Kuhn and his critics. It is assumed that all reasoning is subject to precise and specifiable rules, so that to use words of rational assessment, such as 'probable', 'reasonable', 'satisfactory', 'adequate', 'makes sense', etc., is to apply these rules to the matter in hand. Differences as to what is reasonable, etc., are either about whether certain agreed rules are satisfied in certain cases, in which case they are resolvable, or about what the rules are to be, in which case they are not. The parallel with what moral philosophers have said about words of moral assessment is obvious, and in that context the same paradoxes have resulted. Moral systems or 'ways of life' are made to depend on the choice of basic principles, and the only way of testing the principles is to work out their application in detail and then decide whether one is prepared to accept them

88

having seen what they involve; so that between consistent moral systems there can be no rational choice.

There are at least two difficulties about this conception of reasoning as the following of rules. The first is that of ensuring that we have specified the rules correctly. If the individual is free to stipulate the rules, there is pretty clearly an end of rationality. But if he is not to be free to stipulate, he needs to be able to persuade us that the rules he specifies correspond to those we actually use (or should use) and this involves taking examples of the relevant types of thinking and subjecting them to careful examination. It is necessary to study the reasoning of good reasoners, who are for the most part quite unable to provide the rules by which they reason. Consider, for instance, the sustained debate as to whether historical reasoning consists in the discovery and application of covering laws or the equally controversial issue as to whether all moral reasoning is basically utilitarian. In both cases the issues can be disposed of quite simply by refusing to accept as genuine examples of historical or moral reasoning any cases which cannot be shown to comply with covering-law or utilitarian requirements. Precisely similar intransigence is open to the other side in these debates. But it obviously is intransigence. It is necessary to judge whether the doubtful cases are or are not cases of the type of reasoning in question. There are three possibilities; (*a*) the cases can be made to fit without distortion; (*b*) the cases are not genuine examples of reasoning; (*c*) the rules have not been correctly specified. To decide between these possibilities requires thought. If this exercise of thought has itself to be rule-governed, the question can in turn be raised whether these rules have been correctly specified, and so on *ad infinitum*.

The second difficulty is that, in any case, the rules have to be applied and, since not all cases are straightforward, judgement will be needed in applying them on at least some occasions. Here too a regress seems inevitable unless we recognise a capacity for judgement, which does not itself consist in the following of rules. If, however, being rational involves at some point the exercise of judgement of this sort, there would seem to be no reason in principle why world-views or metaphysical systems should not be subject to rational comparison, however much in practice human limitations may impede the process.

We are now in a position to look back at the earlier stages of the argument in the light of what we have learnt from the discussion of Kuhn's thesis. The original objection was that in such cases as critical exegesis and historical study, rational argument between opposed positions is possible only to the extent that the participants share the same basic conceptual scheme. The comparison with science suggested that this restriction was unnecessary. And, as soon as one begins to entertain this possibility, one is struck by a feature of disagreements within the humanities, which ought perhaps to have been noticed earlier. This is that they often do involve conceptual differences of a kind that may prove troublesome, even when they are not related to conflicting world-views. Kuhn has been criticised for drawing so very sharp a contrast between normal science and science at a time of revolution, when paradigm change is under way. Whatever may be the rights and wrongs of this charge, it is apparent, on reflection, that no such clear distinction can be made in the humanities. Whether or not it is possible to pick out certain periods as being particularly revolutionary (cf. 'The Revolution in Philosophy') the ordinary disagreements of philosophers, historians, literary critics, political theorists appear to involve as a regular feature precisely the sort of misunderstandings which Kuhn takes to be characteristic of periods of scientific revolution. 'Schools of thought' are discernible whose members approach the subject in characteristic ways which normally influence the topics they choose to discuss and the vocabulary in which they discuss them. The review section of any learned journal provides ample evidence of the difficulty scholars often have in understanding one another and their impatience with what they are inclined to regard as the perversity of their opponents. It very frequently happens that scholar A insists on interpreting what scholar B says in terms of the meaning he, A, would give to the terms B uses, rather than that which B himself gives. And in this he is, perhaps, wise, since to adopt B's vocabulary tends to lead insensibly to the acceptance of B's conclusions. In such a situation the reviewer should say explicitly: 'I prefer to discuss the question in terms other than those used by B'. If, however, he does say this, the discussion quickly appears to take on the character of a total impasse.

And it is in fact an impasse so long as the discussion stays at the level at which the misunderstanding has arisen. What is needed is that the disputants should turn their attention to the higher-level question as to the terms in which the original question is best discussed. It is rarely possible entirely to separate the levels, since each scholar will naturally wish to maintain that his theoretical framework is the one whose adoption makes the better sense of what is to be interpreted. They will not make progress so long as they fail to recognise that different presuppositions are involved; but there seems no good reason to deny that rational choice is possible between presuppositions, for they can be judged by their capacity to make sense of all the relevant evidence. There is an essential role for trained judgement in all these rational activities, not least when a choice has to be made between conceptual systems, whether on a large or on a small scale, [25].

It is important, however, not to be led into making the extravagant claim (which is sometimes advanced) that there are no essential differences between religion and science. The present argument, if successful, shows only that, when a choice has to be made between high-level scientific theories or paradigms, the choice cannot be determined wholly by observation or by strict rules of logic; for both the rival paradigms are logically in order and both have access to the same observations and can give an account of them. Yet the choice can be a rational one. However, it is essential to remember that the candidate theories, between which the choice is made, have to be able to satisfy certain conditions, without which they would not be scientific theories at all: conditions which need not be satisfied by philosophical or metaphysical theories or (if these are different) by systems of religious belief.

91

To specify these conditions is a good deal less easy than is generally supposed. Evans claims that scientific assertions differ from religious beliefs in being (i) logically neutral, (ii) comprehensible interpersonally, and (iii) testable by observations.

About (i) there need be no dispute as far as science is concerned. A self-involving assertion, as Evans defines it, is 'one which commits the person who asserts it or accepts it to further action, or which implies that he has an attitude for or against whatever the assertion is about, or which expresses such an attitude' [26]. And it is clear that, although membership of a scientific community involves commitment to an ethic of intellectual honesty, the scientist in putting forward a theory, however much he believes in it, is not thereby committed to an attitude for or against whatever the theory is about or to a future pattern of conduct in relation to it. The problem is, rather, whether, and if so in what sense, religious beliefs are self-involving. To this I shall return later.

About (ii), the claim that scientific assertions are 'comprehensible interpersonally', Evans is compelled to admit a qualification in the case of the social sciences. For the social scientist may sometimes have to take account of the way in which an agent sees his own situation, and the capacity to do this involves a degree of imaginative sympathy which cannot be presumed to be universal. In this respect the social scientist resembles the historian so that the line between the sciences and the humanities becomes somewhat blurred.

In discussing (iii), the requirement for testability by observation, Evans takes full account of the extent to which, as Kuhn has shown, non-observational criteria are relied upon in the choice between paradigms [27].

It is clear that in the paradigm we find science in a form most remote from observational testing, from 'knockdown' falsification or 'conclusive' verification by means of specific observations. Paradigms are very different from restricted generalizations such as 'All the boys in this room right now have blue eyes'. Nevertheless, even Kuhn says that 'observations and experience can and must drastically

92

restrict the range of admissible scientific belief, else there would be no science'. More specifically in his account of the 'anomalies' which force scientific revolutions he notes that a paradigm makes possible a precision of observational expectations which renders it specially sensitive to possible undermining by anomalous observational findings.

Even in the social sciences the requirement remains that evidence, to be admissible, should be capable of being quantified or at least admit of strict controls. And this is not the case in the humanities, let alone in metaphysics or theology. There are, then, fundamental differences between science and religion.

The question is, however, whether the analogies that have been noticed between the role of judgement in science and religion are robbed of their significance by the fact that the scientific theories between which a choice has to be made must first satisfy certain stringent requirements, which cannot be met by religious systems. The whole tenor of our discussion suggests strongly that they are not. There are innumerable examples of non-scientific assertions which are capable of being established or refuted by appeal to experience, but which are not open to strictly scientific test.

It is sometimes argued that in the last resort science, like religion, rests on faith of a kind that is not open to observational test even indirectly. Hare's introduction of the work 'blik' provides the best known and most concisely expressed example of this view. Hare understands by a blik, not a paradigm in Kuhn's sense, but a very general presupposition of all scientific activity. Such a presupposition is not testable by reference to observation, but nevertheless determines the entire direction of scientific inquiry. The suggestion is that religion also depends upon such a blik and that, in both the scientific and the religious case, the adoption of the blik calls for an ultimate decision for which reasons cannot be given. Hare is right to insist on the existence and importance of fundamental concepts, principles and propositions which are not in any ordinary sense subjected to empirical test and are given a regulative function, but it is doubtful whether the thesis can be sustained that there can be no rational choice between such bliks. If we take as an instance of a scientific blik, 'every event has a cause', it is, indeed, true that this principle is not falsified whenever scientists are unable to find a cause for a particular event — they prefer to go on looking for one — nevertheless, as Evans points out, it may be so undermined by failure to verify it that it is abandoned, at least in a specific area of science.

Sometimes an even more general presupposition of science is advanced as being analogous to the theist's faith in God: the principle of induction itself. Here indeed is a presupposition which could not be undermined by observation, because to rely on observation at all would be to presuppose it. Hence it is a presupposition of all empirical inquiry, and theists and atheists both depend upon it. But for this very reason it cannot provide an appropriate parallel to belief in God, for the latter simply does not have the same unchallengeable status in relation to all human thought and action.

The moral which ought to be drawn from the consideration of bliks is that any large-scale theoretical system is highly ramified and includes certain notions which are .of peculiar centrality and importance and cannot be abandoned without the destruction or very radical reform of the entire system. They are not open to straightforward falsification in the way that more peripheral assertions are, because, so long as the system as a whole remains viable, it is always more reasonable instead to abandon or modify less essential claims. But a time may come when they can no longer reasonably be protected in this way. The decision as to when this point has been reached requires the same sort of trained judgement as is demanded by Kuhn's account of the choice between paradigms. Indeed, the only significant difference in this respect between Hare's bliks and Kuhn's paradigms would seem to be that the latter are more restricted in scope. They occur only within science and change with each scientific revolution.

Thus, even if we cannot embrace the sort of apologetic which aims to draw a straight parallel between scientific and

94

religious 'faith', there are important respects in which the analogics which interest us hold. Where there is conflict between two or more scientific paradigms, (a) each can give an account of all the experimental evidence, (b) which of the paradigms gives a better account is something which has to be determined by the judgement of scientists, (c) it is not possible to specify precise rules in accordance with which such decisions are to be made; scientists have to rely on such 'values' (to use Kuhn's word) as consistency, coherence, simplicity, elegance, explanatory power, fertility, (d) these criteria are not themselves relative to particular paradigms. Hence, (e) there is no reason to doubt that choices made with care and competence on the basis of them are rational. And the same may be said *mutatis mutandis* of world-views or metaphysical systems.

If this is so, it provides the answer to the objection raised earlier that with metaphysical systems or world-views, which claim in principle to accommodate all possible experience, there is nothing analgous to the general knowledge of human nature which can to some extent be relied upon in history and literary criticism. There are innumerable points along their periphery at which such systems come into contact with experience and with organised 'bodies of knowledge' and they are bound to take account of them. It is necessary and possible to judge whether, in taking such account, they suppress or distort the facts or whether they respect them and render them more intelligible.

Part III

6 Faith and Knowledge

The position we have now arrived at is that, in its intellectual aspect, traditional Christian theism may be regarded as a world-view or metaphysical system which is in competition with other such systems and must be judged by its capacity to make sense of all the available evidence. It has been argued that it is an error to hold that such expressions as 'make sense of' can only be understood in terms of particular systems, for this is to presuppose what I have been contesting, that reasoning is always to be construed as the following of rules, whose character may to some extent vary from one system to another.

However, even if this account is philosophically unobjectionable, it is liable to be criticised as incomplete, if not inadequate and misleading, from the religious standpoint. It may be felt that it makes of religious belief something quite different from what at its best, or indeed at its most characteristic, we find it to be. Religion, after all, is not primarily a theoretical matter. The typical religious believer does not arrive at his faith by a process of intellectual reflection and is not concerned with testing his beliefs as a scientist or a philosopher is. His faith is not tentative, but unconditional. As Terence Penelhum puts it, 'he considers that he knows'; he writes [1]:

> It has often been pointed out that the adherence which the man of faith has to the doctrines that he proclaims is quite different from the adherence, if that is the word, which someone may have to some explanatory hypothesis, for example in the sciences. In the latter case some proposition is tentatively adopted, and our confidence in it is in proportion to the amount of confirmation it receives. If the evidence seems predominantly against it, it is abandoned. Religious belief is not tentative in this way.

99

Moreover Christianity was, at its inception, 'foolishness to the Greeks' and remains a scandal — something not readily acceptable to the ordinary reasonable man. Indeed there is something almost blasphemous in the notion that Christianity is or ought to be accepted because it 'makes better sense' than alternatives. Not only does it not commend itself to the contemporary world as reasonable and sensible; it ought to challenge and at times condemn our ordinary standards of what is reasonable and sensible. The God of the philosophers is not the God of Abraham, Isaac and Jacob.

These objections are serious ones and only someone with little feeling for religion would take them lightly. In the attempt to meet them it may be possible to clarify and amend the previous account in important respects. I shall endeavour to show that the problem of faith and reason, to which these objections call attention, is very much more complex than is generally supposed and that there is an important sense of 'faith' in which a conflict between faith and reason can occur in secular as well as religious contexts. It is necessary to recognise how far the predicaments of the religious believer and the believer in some non-religious system of thought resemble one another before one can isolate the respects in which they differ.

Let us begin with the contention that Christian theism is not an 'explanatory hypothesis'; where exception is taken to both the noun and the adjective. It is not explanatory and not a hypothesis.

(i) 'Not explanatory'. It is hard to dissociate the question whether theism is in any sense 'explanatory' from prior assumptions as to the sorts of explanations that are possible, and the sorts of role that an explanation of any kind may perform. It would be somewhat perverse to deny that both within a system of religious belief and in the individual's approach to such a system there appear what look like explanations or demands for explanation. The perplexed individual who asks 'What is this all for, what does it mean?' is ostensibly looking for some explanation of the 'changes and chances of this transitory life'. And if he becomes persuaded that all these things have a purpose in the

100

providence of God, then it would seem that he has found an explanation. The refusal to admit that explanation really is involved stems either from philosophical inhibitions upon the use of the word in this sort of context or from a tendency, common among theologians, to associate 'explanation' with an approach that is narrowly intellectual.

There is an enormous philosophical literature about explanation, and any attempt to meet the difficulties here can only be tentative. As has already been pointed out [2], it has to be conceded that theological explanations cannot be of a scientific kind. In so far as they succeed in achieving a gain in intelligibility they do so not by suggesting a hypothesis from which deductions are made which are subject to strict experimental test, but by placing what has to be explained in a fresh conceptual framework in relation to which answers are possible to questions of a different kind to those asked in the sciences.

The theistic framework is built round the notion of a supreme creative will, conceived on the analogy of personal choice. For the analogy to have any force it must be the case both that explanations in terms of purpose are not reducible to explanations in terms of inductive regularities, and that sense can be made of the notion of a supreme creative will. But these conditions have to be satisfied if traditional Christian theism is to be stated at all, whether or not it has an explanatory function. If they can be satisfied and theism can be intelligibly stated, there is no further reason why the theistic scheme should be denied the explanatory function which it purports to have. Moreover, as soon as it is recognised that the sorts of explanations it provides are characteristically those afforded by the ascription of purposes to persons, the way is open for a resolution of the second difficulty: the association of explanation with the narrowly intellectual. Flew has been quoted earlier [3]:

Nor will it do to recognise that of a whole series of arguments each individually is defective, but then to urge that nevertheless in sum they comprise an impressive case; perhaps adding as a sop to the Cerberus of criticism that

101

this case is addressed to the whole personality and not merely to the philosophical intellect.

If the appeal to 'the whole personality' is merely a device to disarm the 'philosophical intellect' it deserves the scorn which Flew directs upon it. But the possibility has to be faced that an intellectual understanding of the Christian case may in fact make certain demands on the whole personality, as may be seen by contrasting the extent to which personal qualities are involved in the work of a natural scientist and of a historian or a moralist.

Although, as has often been insisted [4], natural science can only be developed in a community of scientists who acknowledge certain ethical demands, these personal qualities are needed only to ensure that the individual's scientific work conforms to the required intellectual standards. In the execution of the work itself there are many features of the scientist's personality which are irrelevant to his success. The point is well made by Evans in his discussion of the requirement that scientific assertions should be interpersonally comprehensible [5]:

If a man has sufficient intelligence and scientific training he should be able to understand a particular scientific assertion regardless of his personal attitudes concerning what the assertion is about, and regardless of his moral, aesthetic, or spiritual appreciation of what the assertion is about. The conditions for understanding are scientific, not intimately personal. For example, let us suppose that John Brown does not understand what is meant by 'light travels in straight lines'. If he has enough brain power and if he studies enough physics he should be able to understand the assertion. This understanding should be possible whether or not light is something that matters tremendously to him, whether or not he is a self-centred or an altruistic person, whether or not he has ever contemplated a beam of light with the eye of an artist. The conditions for understanding a particular scientific assertion are independent of these variable personal factors. It is a matter of intelligence and scientific training.

102

The same is evidently not the case with most work in the humanities or even in the social sciences [6]. The individual scholar's moral, aesthetic or spiritual appreciation directly affects, in many cases, his capacity to understand what he is talking about and to make sound judgements about it. To take an extreme example, a psychopath who lacked entirely the capacity to put himself imaginatively in someone else's place and consider his interests would be unable to appreciate a wide range of human motives; he could scarcely become a historian. Yet we do not normally regard ourselves, in considering the humanities, as compelled to choose between denying that they provide us with explanations at all or stigmatising them as 'purely intellectual'.

There are many people who lack any form of religious sensitivity, who have never at any time worshipped, or prayed or felt at all tempted to worship or pray, whose response to religious music or religious architecture has always been purely aesthetic, who at no time have experienced any radical dissatisfaction with themselves and their accepted ends or any sense of impenetrable mystery. It is inevitable that such persons should be defective in their appreciation of theism. This is not to say (as some religious apologists wrongly do) that positive commitment to a religious position is a necessary condition of understanding it. Critics of Christianity who are united in their rejection of it vary greatly in the degree of sympathetic imagination with which they treat its claims, and some of them show a profounder understanding of Christian mysteries than do many theologians. Individuals vary enormously in the use they can make of a given amount of experience, and we cannot be sure that such persons have had more 'religious experience' (or what purports to be such) than others; only that they have made better use of it.

A man cannot be in a position to understand Christian theism who does not appreciate that in that system God is the being who is to be worshipped, and he cannot understand that unless he has some notion what worshipping is like. But to recognise that God, if he exists, is to be worshipped is not the same as to believe that there is a God. And to believe that there is a God (who is to be worshipped) is not in itself to

103

worship. A man who claimed to believe in God and did not worship him could be criticised as insincere or hypocritical or irrational or in some other way defective in his attitude; but it would not follow that he did not believe in God, at least in the minimal sense of believing that there is a God. Nor would any degree of 'self-involvement' however serious or 'ultimate' amount to belief in God, as Christians think of him, if what the believer believed in, as expressed in his words or his actions, did not sufficiently conform to the Christian conception of God. So that self-involvement is not only not a necessary condition of belief in God; it is not a sufficient condition either.

(ii) 'Not a hypothesis'. Part of the trouble here is that the use of 'hypothesis' readily suggests that religious belief is 'hypothetical' in the sence of tentative and provisional. And it is clear that, in this sense, the religious believer does not normally treat his faith as a hypothesis. It enters too deeply into his whole understanding of life and the world and his attitude to them. Moreover the word 'hypothesis' does not do justice to the richness and complexity, the mystery and the profundity of religious belief. To the extent that comparison with natural science is appropriate, traditional Christian theism is more like the entire corpus of contemporary physics than it is like a single physical theory.

However, although these remarks about the phenomenology of religious belief may lead us to qualify the use of the word 'hypothesis' in this context, the underlying problem is more than a merely terminological one. The substantial objection to the account so far given is that, when every allowance has been made for the 'richness' of a system of religious belief, it follows from that account that the individual's assent to his religious belief ought to be merely tentative and conditional. But Christian faith is, and ought to be, unconditional. Our mistake has been, in Bultmann's words, to 'substitute a *Weltanschauung* for faith' [7]. If religion stands in need of a theoretical justification, such as in outline I have attempted to provide, then it must be more or less plausible. It may become reasonable to accept Christian theism indeed, but to the extent and only to the extent that

104

'the evidence' justifies it. Religious belief, so understood, has to be regarded as open to revision or even to refutation if there is a sufficient accumulation of contrary evidence. It is not enough, in reply to this criticism, to point out that a hypothesis need not be treated as if it were hypothetical; if it is a hypothesis which is open to any degree of doubt, it ought to be treated as hypothetical, and if what religious believers characteristically do is correctly describable as 'treating unconfirmed hypotheses as if they were not hypothetical' their position is epistemologically and, indeed, ethically unsound

The objection may be restated as follows. Any account of Christian theism which represents it as the product of a cumulative case of the kind suggested allows the possibility that some rival world-view might in the end turn out to be the true one. Hence the Christian, in so far as he is intellectually honest, must always think it possible that he is mistaken. He may, psychologically speaking, shut out this possibility from his mind, but this must be regarded as intellectual and moral weakness. The account, therefore, is bound to dismiss as uncharacteristic or stigmatise as improper the unconditional commitment of the man of faith and his conviction that, in some sense, he knows.

It is commonly assumed, therefore, that the committed character of faith can be explained and justified in two ways only: either faith is adherence to propositions which are immune to rational test; or it is a form of knowledge. We have seen reason to reject the first alternative; the second remains to be considered.

Two recent writers have developed the idea of faith as a form of knowledge, Penelhum and Hick. In each case what is insisted on is that, to use Penelhum's words, 'there seems no other appropriate way of speaking of the mode of experience characteristic of the great formative figures of the Christian tradition' [8].

Perhaps God exists, and perhaps not. Philosophy will not tell us. But *if* God exists, then Abraham and Isaiah and

105

Peter and Paul *knew* that he does. And, if he does not, they had everything that goes to make up knowledge except the truth of the proposition held to [9].

Penelhum is endeavouring to provide an account of religious faith which will be acceptable to both theists and atheists. To say without qualification that the great religious figures knew that God exists would imply that God does exist, and this is at issue between theists and atheists. Therefore he uses the expression 'consider themselves to know'. He believes that there is in fact no way of proving either that God does or does not exist that is available to both parties. There are 'revelatory phenomena' but they are not probative to anyone who does not already know that God exists.

He rejects the position he calls 'radical theological non-naturalism', according to which there are no non-theistic statements, which, if they were known to be true, would serve to prove God's existence or any other theistic proposition. That is to say, he does not embrace any of the varieties of conceptual relativism I have discussed earlier. Indeed he is prepared to claim that the gospel story, culminating in the Resurrection, would provide us with the probative revelatory phenomena we need, if only we could know the phenomena to have occurred. But, as it is, we depend upon the reports of witnesses and this makes it always rational for someone to dispute them.

The probative status of the primary events of the tradition, given the person-relativity of proof, is therefore confined to those who witnessed the events (or those who have other theistic knowledge which makes it irrational to doubt that they occurred as recorded). For others, the deadlock appears to remain [10].

The state of mind of the man of faith is

analogous to that of someone who is in direct personal contact with another, greater, person . . . . If it should turn

106

out that the other person does not in fact exist, and that the one who thought he knew him has been the victim of illusion, it will still be true that he considered himself to know that he had dealings with the other. And to consider oneself to know this is to consider oneself to know at least some of the critical propositions about the other person that one could not fail to know if one indeed were in converse with him [11].

Hick speaks in much the same terms. Of the great religious figures he says, 'God was known to them as a dynamic will interacting with their own wills, a sheer given reality . . . not an inferred entity but an experienced reality . . . They were vividly aware of being in his presence' [12]. Whether or not this state of mind is to be identified with faith (and this is something that will need to be considered later) there is no doubt that it is characteristic of the leading figures of the Judaeo-Christian tradition. This 'sense of the presence of God', as has been argued earlier, plays an essential part in the case for Christian theism. But it cannot stand alone. It is open to alternative interpretations. As Hick himself acknowledges, 'there is no item offered as theistic or anti-theistic evidence which cannot be absorbed by a mind operating with different presuppositions into the contrary view' [13]. Hence the correctness of any particular interpretation cannot be guaranteed simply by the experience itself, but relies on a conceptual framework which draws support also from other, independent, evidence. In the absence of·a framework of theology it would not be possible to claim that the encounter is with God as Christians conceive him. This emerges clearly in Hepburn's dialogue between the 'encounter theologian', White, and the philosophical critic, Black. Black asks White who it is that he encounters:

White: I mean 'God the Father Almighty, Maker of Heaven and Earth . . . .' Black: All right. Now what I should very much like to know is whether all this information about God is given in the immediacy of the encounter, and if so, how . . . How could one know *immediately* and certainly that God was Father Almighty, or that he made the heavens and earth? . . . [14].

Hick endeavours to turn the flank of this argument by insisting that, for the great primary religious figures, belief in the reality of God is not comparable to an explanatory hypothesis with a good deal of theoretical content, but rather to a perceptual belief such as our ordinary belief in the perceived natural world [15].

> If this is so, it is appropriate that the religious man's belief in the reality of God should be no more provisional than his belief in the reality of the physical world. The situation is in each case that, given the experience which he has and which is part of him, he cannot help accepting as 'there' such aspects of his environment as he experiences. He cannot help believing either in the reality of the material world which he is conscious of inhabiting, or of the personal divine presence to which his mode of living is a free response. And I have been suggesting that it is as reasonable for him to hold and act upon the one belief as the other.

Hick concedes that there are differences between the two situations, notably that, whereas we all cannot help believing in the external world, comparatively few enjoy an equally compelling religious experience; and this may suggest that those few are deluded. But, he insists, here as in other perceptual situations the mere possibility of delusion is not enough to warrant scepticism; there must be positive grounds for impugning the judgement of the religious believer and 'the general intelligence and exceptionally high moral quality of the great religious figures clashes with any analysis of their experience in terms of abnormal psychology' [16].

The chief difficulty with this comparison is one that Hick half recognises, but fails adequately to meet. As he remarks, 'It is a basic truth in or presupposition of our language that it is rational or sane to believe in the reality of the external

108

world that we inhabit in common with other people, and irrational and insane not to do so' [17]. It is not simply that we find ourselves under a psychological compulsion to believe in a world of things and persons; there is no coherent alternative. It is for this reason that the sceptical argument from illusion fails. In order to recognise an illusion for what it is we have to assume that our perceptual judgements are generally reliable; and this is an assumption which, because of the centrality of things and persons in any conceivable world-view, we necessarily make. So long as the existence of God is presupposed, it will be true that, in a precisely similar way, we shall not be able to use the possibility that some 'encounters' with God are illusory as a reason for denying that a particular one is genuine. But the presupposition in this case is one that can be challenged and, therefore, requires a defence. Hick provides some of the ingredients for such a defence but does not render it unnecessary.

Both Hick and Penelhum (particularly the latter) draw so sharp a contrast between the epistemological position of the 'great religious figures' and of the atheist that it becomes a problem what to say about those who are in neither situation, or who are in process of moving in one direction or the other. If there is in fact deadlock between those who 'consider themselves to know' that there is a God and those who consider themselves to know that there is not, what are we to make of those who believe without considering that they know? For every 'great religious figure' there are innumerable others who adopt a religious interpretation of life and live their lives on the basis of it, but whose sense of the presence of God is at best fitful and sometimes entirely lacking. Yet their faith (if such it is) is not, in their judgement, without rational support. They recognise that such support would be stronger if they were able to claim to know God in some direct fashion and they are impressed by the witness of those who can make this claim, but, if asked to justify the faith that is in them, they are not wholly without recourse.

If the ordinary believer is not in as weak a position as the Hick-Penelhum theory would suggest, the position of the

109

man who considers himself to know is, as we have seen, not as invulnerable as they make it out to be. For to the extent that there is a genuine possibility that the 'sense of the presence of God' might be shown to be illusory, it cannot be maintained even by someone who experiences it, that the interpretation he places upon that experience is correct beyond reasonable doubt. If, then, it is a necessary condition of knowing that p, that there is not the remotest chance of not p being true, he does not know that there is a God [18].

Since, therefore, it is the case both that experience cannot guarantee the correctness of the interpretation placed upon it, and that there are in the field rival interpretations with some degree of rational support, it would seem that even the individual who enjoys the experience will need to rely on the support of reasons other than the evidence of the experience itself. He will, in fact, need to draw upon an entire religious tradition in order to make his unique contribution to it. And for this to be possible the tradition must possess its own independent weight.

If what I have been saying is correct, it would seem that, for one sense of 'know' at least, Penelhum is mistaken in claiming that, should it turn out that there is no God, the great religious figures 'had everthing that goes to make up knowledge except the truth of the proposition held to'. For, even if God does exist, the grounds for believing now that he exists may fall short of being conclusive. Hick by implication concedes this in his account of 'eschatological verification', in which he envisages a state of affairs after death in which men enjoy, as they cannot now, an experience of the fulfilment of Christ's purpose for themselves, and an experience of communion with God as disclosed in Christ, such as would remove all rational doubt about the existence of God.

If it is true of the doctrine of God that it cannot, at least in this present life, be put beyond all rational doubt, even for those who claim to be directly aware of his presence, and that even those who lack this direct awareness can have some grounds for accepting it, it is even more obviously true of other Christian doctrines, more especially those that involve historical claims. That the God whom the saints encounter is

110

the God who was incarnate in Jesus Christ is a claim that depends for its truth on the historical facts of the life and death of Jesus. Penelhum is right in insisting that it makes an important difference to one's assessment of the historical evidence in relation to the doctrine of the Incarnation, whether one does or does not presuppose the existence of God, but even for those who have, as he puts it, 'theistic knowledge' the assertion that God revealed himself in these events could be seriously impugned by historical inquiry, and with it any beliefs about God and his purposes attributable to the authority of Christ; and for those who lack 'theistic knowledge' but who hold that there are independent grounds of some substance for believing in God, the record of the Gospels, in so far as it is believed on balance to deserve credit, may properly be the vehicle of revelation [19].

The sharpness of the contrast which Penelhum draws may be due in part to an assumption which appears to underlie his entire discussion: that rational conviction must come through proof or not at all. The possibility that the case for theism might be of the cumulative sort we have been considering scarcely comes into the reckoning. Hence the total impasse which he finds inevitable between those who have theistic knowledge and those who lack it and his unwillingness to countenance the possibility that 'revelatory phenomena' may have probative force. This is all the more surprising in that he does not rest his case on any variety of conceptual relativism, even though his language sometimes suggests it. So far as he can see, the revelatory phenomena which have actually occurred might have been probative; they just happen not to be; and, as it is, they all have precisely the same degree of non-probativeness. But that this should be so is surely very odd. If there are phenomena, such as conspicuous sanctity, which, if there is a God, provide strong evidence that there is, then the fact that they exist must be acknowledged to give some rational support to theism even in the eyes of those who claim no independent knowledge that God exists; stronger support than is provided, for example, by some individual's transient sense of his own finitude, although this too is not entirely without weight. And both of these are to be contrasted with some apparently pointless disaster which, left unexplained, must tend to undermine theism.

Nevertheless the emphasis placed by these writers upon the claim of at least some religious figures, and those among the greatest, to enjoy some kind of personal relationship with God is of immense importance. They must be right in insisting that, if theism is true, such men can be said to know God and not merely to have given their assent to a theistic metaphysic; and that even those who would not claim to know God in this way nevertheless rely on him and trust in him in a manner that is not merely tentative and provisional.

How, then, can these truths be reconciled with what has appeared to be the conclusion of the present discussion: that there is an important sense of 'know' in which even the 'great religious figures' cannot be said to know that there is a God (let alone other Christian doctrines) so long as it remains a genuine possibility that some non-theistic interpretation of their experience might turn out to be true?

The answer would seem to be that the problem has been posed in terms of false alternatives. Hick is anxious to avoid being committed to a God who is merely an 'inferred entity' and he fears that he would be committed to this if he were to regard theistic belief as in any sense an explanatory hypothesis. Since he assumes that to admit the possibility of argument about the genuineness of the sense of the presence of God would be to reduce it to the level of a hypothesis, he has no choice but to place it beyond reach of rational criticism. Either God is at best an inferred entity and faith in God no more than acceptance of a hypothesis; or God is an experienced realitiy about which rational doubt is, at least for the one who experiences, impossible. That these are not, however, exhaustive alternatives can be seen from two illustrations. The first is a straightforward perceptual one.

In a ship at sea in stormy weather, the officer of the watch reports a lighthouse on a certain bearing. The navigating officer says he cannot have seen a lighthouse, because his

112

reckoning puts him a hundred miles away from the nearest land. He must have seen a waterspout or a whale blowing or some other marine phenomenon which can be taken for a lighthouse. The officer of the watch is satisfied he must have made a mistake. Shortly afterwards, however, the lookout reports land on the starboard bow. The navigating officer, still confident in his working, says it must be cloud — and it is indeed very difficult to distinguish cloud from land in these conditions. But then a second cloud-looking-like-land or land-looking-like-cloud appears on another bearing. It really does begin to look as if the navigator might be out in his reckoning. He has, perhaps, underestimated the current, or his last star sight was not as good as he thought it was. The reported sightings are consistent with one another and indicate that he is approaching land.

If it is wartime and the coast is hostile, he had better assume that he is where the sightings place him, and get away from it quickly. It would be nice to be surer, but in the circumstances it would be prudent to act on the hypothesis which gives him the stronger reason for action. (Perhaps there is a moral to be drawn here for the ethics of belief. If so, now is not the time to draw it). The point at present is simply that the question whether there was a lighthouse there and the question whether the officer of the watch saw it or saw something else, or just imagined that he saw it, can only be answered in relation to some overall appraisal of the situation. The navigator's original appraisal, based on his dead reckoning, led him to say there was no lighthouse and the officer of the watch did not see it; and this was reasonable enough at that stage. But the other reports, although their evidential value, taken singly, is as slight and as controversial as the first, do cumulatively amount to a convincing case for reading the whole situation differently. However, it does not in the least follow that, because the lighthouse hypothesis required the support of this sort of reasoning before it could properly be accepted, the lighthouse was for the lookout merely an inferred entity and not an experienced reality. Indeed that it was an experienced reality is precisely what the argument indicated.

113

Of course there are no doubts as to whether there are such things as lighthouses, whereas there are doubts as to whether there is a God. To allow for this difference another illustration may be developed from Wisdom's parable of the Invisible Gardener [20].

Two men return to their long-neglected garden and find signs of cultivation which lead one of them to say that a gardener must still be working there. However no gardener is ever observed at work although a careful watch is kept. This man then says that there must be an invisible and intangible gardener, while the other denies it.

As Wisdom actually presents his parable no one ever sees or claims to see the gardener. He is for both men an inferred entity in the quite straightforward sense that his existence is posited to explain the otherwise puzzling phenomenon of the partly cultivated garden. If the gardener were an ordinary, visible gardener and someone met him, there is a quite obvious sense in which he would become for that person an experienced reality and no longer just an inferred entity. Suppose now we modify the parable. The man in the garden does not claim to have (literally) seen and heard the gardener, but he does claim to have been vividly aware of the presence of the gardener. Not only that, but he hears or claims to hear a voice (an internal voice perhaps, but not, so far as he can tell, his own), and this voice explains to him what the gardener is trying to do with the garden (on the lines, perhaps, of the Parable of the Wheat and the Tares; was this the origin of Wisdom's parable?). Surely his experience is different from that of the man for whom the invisible gardener is still merely an inferred entity.

It is tempting to reply to this that of course his experience is different; but his experience cannot be self-authenticating. Hence the most he is entitled to do is to put forward the hypothesis that he was in the presence of the gardener, heard the gardener's voice, etc. And this means that for this man too the gardener is still, logically speaking, an inferred entity.

Now it seems to me that Hick should concede at once that the experiences in question are not self-authenticating. It is only in the light of some overall theory that the man in the

114

garden could be entitled to claim that what he experienced really was (amounted to) being in the presence of and hearing the voice of the gardener. Or, to put it another way, it is only if he cannot find a better explanation of the phenomenon that he is entitled to claim this; but if he cannot, then he is entitled to claim it.

Similarly with claims to be directly aware of the presence of God. It is assumed that claims to direct awareness of God must be either self-authenticating or disguised inferences. Since they are clearly not self-authenticating they must be disguised inferences. I suggest a third possibility: that they are what they purport to be, cases of direct awareness, but that the claim that this is what they are relies upon there being a theory or conceptual scheme in terms of which the claim can be adequately defended.

I do not think that Hick need dissent from this. He uses the word 'inference' in a broad sense and what I am proposing to distinguish from inference he regards as a sort of inference. He tends to regard as inferred and hence as a hypothesis any conclusion which falls short of demonstrative certainty. I am suggesting that even when someone is not in any ordinary sense advancing a hypothesis, but rather claiming direct acquaintance, it is proper to ask the question 'how else would you explain?', and the degree of confidence he is justified in placing in his interpretation of the experience is related to its plausibility in comparison with the alternatives. To take an extreme case, if it were conclusively demonstrated that the concept of God is self-contradictory, then we could be sure that someone was wrong in supposing that he was conscious of being in the presence of God. If, all things considered, a Freudian account of religious belief provided a fairly convincing explanation of this individual's state of mind, it would become correspondingly unlikely that he was conscious of being in the presence of God. If, however, evidence accumulated, as it conceivably might do after death in the manner of Hick's 'eschatological verification', of such power as to render alternative interpretations enormously improbable, then we should be irrational not to accept his account of what he had experienced. The reason why I do not want

115

to call this mode of reasoning 'inference' is that it tempts philosophers, wrongly as it seems to me, to ignore, indeed to reject, the perfectly good distinction between an inferred entity and an experienced reality.

There is, then, if I am right, no reason for denying that, if theism is true, there are men who are directly aware of encounter with God in the same way that in Wisdom's parable, as I developed it, if there was an invisible gardener, one of the men did actually encounter him. The question which was up for decision about the man's experience was whether it did or did not amount to a direct awareness of the gardener; or, to use Hick's terminology, whether the gardener was or was not for him an experienced reality. In neither case was there any question of the gardener's being for him merely an inferred entity. In the one case he was more that an inferred entity; in the other case the experience would have no evidential value at all so that, in relation to that experience, the gardener was not even an inferred entity.

However, the original problem still remains. If it is possible at all that what is taken by those who experience it to be direct encounter with God is not indeed what it purports to be, and that some alternative interpretation of their experience might in the end prove to be correct, then, it may be urged, the 'theory or conceptual scheme' in terms of which their interpretation can be rationally defended is not known to be true. It can, at best, be more or less well supported and thus deserving only of tentative or provisional adherence. And this places the would-be defender of the rationality of theistic belief in a dilemma. For, to the extent that he attempts to indicate how faith can be rationally defended, he is led to characterise faith in a way that fails to satisfy the religious mind; but if he portrays faith as it characteristically operates in the life and thought of believers, he describes something inevitably incommensurate with the only sort of justification that is available.

116

7 Rationality and Commitment

The problem before us is that, if systems of religious belief require and admit of rational justification, as has been argued, they ought only to be accepted more or less provisionally; yet the religious believer characteristically gives whole-hearted assent to his beliefs. Either, then, our account of religious faith is inadequate or such faith has to be condemned as inherently irrational. At this stage in the argument, as on earlier occasions, it is worth noticing that it is not only in connection with religious belief that the problem arises. Mention has been made earlier of the analogies that exist between systems of religious and political belief. Both are, characteristically, involved in a 'form of life'. If we take, for example, liberal democracy, we find that, at the level of theory, it is enormously complex, and in practice it can work successfully only if the institutions in which it is embodied are supported by the appropriate attitudes and skills of a very wide range of types of people. The apparatus of representative government and of the courts of law in a liberal society depends for its continued effectiveness on the continuing trust of the great majority. It is reasonable to suppose that underlying all this are certain conceptions of the value of freedom, equality and justice, which in their turn are associated with certain beliefs about the nature and potentialities of men. These are rarely made articulate and the task of making them articulate is of extraordinary difficulty. Nor is full agreement reached about these matters among political theorists, even among those who would unhesitatingly call themselves liberal democrats. Yet it would be misleading to say of the ordinary Englishman, however well-educated, that he accepts liberal democracy as a hypothesis. The assumptions underlying it enter too deeply into his activities and attitudes for this way of

117

speaking to be appropriate. The institutions under which he lives and has been brought up, and the ideas associated with them, have made the Englishman a certain sort of man. His basic political convictions are more like prejudice than hypothesis (in Edmund Burke's sense of the word 'prejudice' [1]).

It does not follow that liberal democracy requires no theoretical justification and admits of none. It has an intellectual structure, difficult though it may be to analyse it and controversial though any proffered analysis may be; and it has been subjected to radical criticism, notably by Marxists. It would be a bold man who would say that there is not the remotest chance of these criticisms being well-founded. On the continent of Europe political discussion among intellectuals is habitually conducted in Marxist terms even by those who are not committed Marxists, and the Anglo-Saxon tradition of liberal democratic theory is not regarded as a serious option. This state of affairs will not surprise professional philosophers, who know how very differently their subject is approached on either side of the Channel. In such a situation it is not enough to claim that one's own familiar system works, for so, to a greater or lesser extent, do the alternatives. What is called for is a theoretical analysis and justification of the liberal democratic system [2].

The theory of liberal democracy is controversial in the quite straightforward sense that there are many men of undoubted rationality who do not accept it. Yet, as we have seen, it is not the case that the ordinary man who believes in democracy entertains it simply as a hypothesis which he is prepared to relinquish should experience begin to cast doubt upon it. This is because it is so much part of himself that to give it up and become, say, a card-carrying member of the Communist Party would involve a thoroughgoing conversion. Nor is it even reasonable to maintain that he ought to be ready to give it up if he finds himself unable to provide a theoretical justification of it or defend it rationally against its critics. Most of us would be hard pressed to hold our own against a well-trained Marxist. No doubt this is partly because

118

it is not the ordinary man's job; he is entitled to a large extent to take it on authority, the sort of authority that is exercised almost imperceptibly by the whole way of life in which he is involved. But it is not clear, either, that it is incumbent upon the political theorist who is a liberal democrat to give up his convictions whenever he is unable to counter a critic's arguments. His faith in liberal democracy may rightly suffice to assure him that he, or someone else, will find the answer in the end.

A second analogy might be provided by the philosophical problem of the freedom of the will. Dr Johnson remarked 'We know our will is free and there's an end on't', and in this he speaks for most of us in our everyday concerns. Nevertheless it can scarcely be denied that the question of determinism is a controversial one. Given the extent of the disagreement on this issue it would be rash to declare that there was not the remotest chance of determinism, in one or other of its forms, turning out to be true. Should it do so, there is a further controversial question as to whether the denial of determinism is implied in our usual ascriptions of moral and legal responsibility. Ayer in his lecture 'Man as a Subject for Science' takes the view that whether human choices can in principle be predicted is a question about which not enough is known to enable us to decide [3]:

The strength of the determinists lies in the fact that there seems to be no reason why the reign of law should break down at this point, though this is an argument which seemed more convincing in the age of classical physics than it does today. The strength of the indeterminists lies in the fact that the specific theories which alone could vindicate or indeed give any substance to their opponents' case have not yet been more than sketched, though this not to say they never will be. Until such theories are properly elaborated and tested, I think that there is little more about this topic that can be usefully said.

He remains agnostic on the question whether, if determinism were true, our ideas of freedom and responsibility would or should be affected; though he admits that most people think they would be: 'I am, indeed, strongly inclined to think that our ordinary ideas of freedom and responsibility are very muddle-headed: but, for what they are worth, they are also very firmly held. It would not be at all easy to estimate the social consequences of discarding them' [4].

Now what, in view of all this, is or should be the status of those strongly-held 'ordinary ideas of freedom and responsibility'? I think we can take it that the possibility cannot be ruled out that some form of determinism is true, and that it is incompatible with our ordinary ideas of freedom and responsibility. If so, there is a sense in which Dr Johnson was wrong. Not only do we not know that we are able to choose freely; we do not know that we are responsible in the sense required for morality as we normally understand it. What, then, is to be our attitude to that entire area of life to which these notions appear to be central? To what extent and in what degree are we to treat ourselves and others as morally responsible? Are we to respond to people as moral beings whose actions and attitudes can properly be assessed from a moral point of view or are we not? Important features of our habitual way of thinking and acting depend upon our doing so.

I shall not attempt to set out the relationships between the concepts of freedom, responsibility, justice, duty, and so forth, which, as well as being controversial, are extremely subtle and complex. All that is necessary for the argument at this point is that the relationships exist and that it is a genuine possibility that the entire conceptual scheme in which they are involved may stand in need of more or less drastic revision.

Let us call 'naturalists' those who accept determinism and regard man as wholly a 'subject for science'; and 'humanists' those who believe that man's freedom is something not to be exhausted by scientific research. For either party the existence of the other as a body of reasonable men is enough to introduce an element of theoretical doubt, in the face of which a variety of attitudes is possible. Among (for example) humanists will be some who are altogether untouched and

120

untroubled by the theoretical problem. Like Dr Johnson, 'They know their will is free and there's an on't'. If it were represented to them that the issue is a controversial one and that the most they are entitled to do is to regard the freedom of the will and its associated notions as a hypothesis which might turn out to be false and which, therefore, should command only provisional assent, they would reply in the manner of Hick when he says of the great religious figures, 'They acted and spoke as men who were vividly conscious of being in the presence of God ... who was not to them an inferred entity but an experienced reality'. They would claim, in effect, that to use Samuel Alexander's phrase, they 'enjoy' freedom and 'enjoy' the sort of intercourse with their fellows which only makes sense if humanism is true. In this they would be right. But they would be wrong if they regarded this 'enjoyment' as entirely self-authenticating, so that it could be relied upon to put naturalism totally out of court.

Others, however, might be aware of, and profoundly worried by, the challenge of naturalism. In constant contact with people who either were naturalists or who adopted naturalism as a methodological principle in their scientific work, they might no longer find it possible to 'enjoy' quite unselfconsciously the experience of freedom and to employ spontaneously in their assessments of people those moral concepts which are associated with it. They might be tempted, when confronted by extraordinary unselfishness or unusual malice, to withhold the moral praise or condemnation that would 'come naturally' to them and think only in terms of the social utility or otherwise of the conduct in question. I do not think I am painting a wholly imaginary picture. If one reads a serious modern novel and then goes back to one of the great Victorians, one is often struck by the presence in the Victorians, and the absence in the moderns, of the emphasis upon individual responsibility. And I fancy that over twenty years of tutorials in moral philosophy I have found it increasingly difficult to assume, as Sir David Ross used to do, a 'common moral consciousness', particularly in relation to such notions as desert and

121

retributive justice. For the humanist exposed to such temptations it requires something like a conscious and continuous act of faith to go on applying his old standards and seeing his 'world' as he used to see it. In so far as he does so, it is certainly not an arbitrary 'leap of faith'; there are good grounds for maintaining the humanist position, but not, if I am right, wholly unassailable ones.

The point of introducing these analogies in the first instance was to help deal with the objection that the account previously given would require religious belief to be tentative and provisional, whereas at its best and most characteristic it is firm and unwavering. I have tried to suggest, with the aid of them, that wherever there is a complex system of beliefs in terms of which a man interprets a wide range of his experience and in relation to which he lives his life, it is the case both that the system stands in need of rational justification and that it is not, and ought not to be, in any ordinary sense of the word, adopted by him as a hypothesis, in a merely tentative and provisional fashion.

Why is this? The answer may become clearer if we consider the conditions in which a theoretical system of any kind develops. A theoretical system develops through its capacity to deal with counter-examples and, as Kuhn has pointed out in connection with natural science, these are never lacking. The problems of the scientist or any other theorist are set him in just this way. He attempts to solve them in a variety of ways: by modifying the main body of the system, or by leaving it intact and introducing supplementary hypotheses, or through other devices. It is only when such devices have repeatedly failed and there is available an alternative system which gives promise of more satisfactory results, that the scientist is prepared to abandon his original position. Hence a 'principle of tenacity' is needed to ensure that the scientist is not prematurely diverted from a promising course of inquiry.

Moreover, a complex theoretical system is not, and could not be, the creation of a single individual, though some outstanding individual may well have been a dominant influence in its formation. It is obvious that political, moral

122

and religious conceptual systems are products of a community, which is responsible for transmitting its beliefs and the language in which they are expressed. Although genuine originality occurs, it does not and cannot consist in the repudiation of the whole of an existing tradition. However radical the transformation it effects, it maintains a certain continuity with the past. It is only in this way that succeeding generations can avoid the impossible task of constructing an entire language and culture from scratch. For this reason education has to take the form of inducting the young into an existing tradition as a necessary condition of equipping them to criticise and amend it. An education can be wholly traditional; it cannot be wholly critical. This is true even of natural science which is the critical discipline *par excellence*. No one can get into a position to make an original contribution to science without having first submitted himself to a thoroughgoing professional training in the course of which he necessarily has to take a good deal on authority. Kuhn and Polanyi (among others) have drawn attention to the internal strains which this process imposes on the scientific community. There has to be a continual tension between tradition and criticism, in which it belongs to a healthy tradition to encourage and respond to criticism, and criticism, to be effective, must recognise and respect tradition.

For this reason the individual scientist's situation in relation to the body of accepted scientific knowledge is quite different from his situation in relation to a particular hypothesis, which he has formulated and is trying to test. Such a hypothesis he will indeed be prepared to accept or reject in accordance with experimental findings, when suitably repeated by himself and others. He can, so to speak, take it or leave it: and whichever he does, in normal cases, will not profoundly affect the structure of his science. This is the situation we generally have in mind when we think of someone treating something as a hypothesis. Since it represents the normal situation of the research scientist it is natural to take it as the paradigm of the scientific attitude [5]. But the scientist cannot, and should not, adopt

123

this 'take it or leave it' attitude to the main body of, e.g., physics.

With regard to that it seems clear that he is justified in accepting it without an exhaustive inquiry into its credentials. Indeed such an inquiry is a practical impossibility. Yet it would be wrong to say that he simply takes its truth for granted. He has good reasons, all but unassailable, for assuming its truth; at least there are good reasons and, though he may not be able to rehearse them, he is not unreasonable in being confident that they exist. Of course it may turn out that, in the future, more or less far-reaching changes are required, but this possibility, although in the light of past experience it amounts to a probability, scarcely warrants any diminution in his present confidence.

So long as no actual alternative system is on offer, his only hope of progress is to proceed on the basis of what is currently accepted. He accepts it, of course, not uncritically but nevertheless in such a manner that the area over which he himself can be effectively critical is limited, and even within that area he cannot criticise everything at once.

It follows from this that, whatever logicians may say, there is a clear sense in which the scientist's acceptance of the main body of his science cannot be 'tentative and provisional'. It is a condition of the possibility of progress that it should not be. His attitude is certainly not one of 'blind faith' but neither is it one of assured knowledge, if this is taken to imply that there is no chance that any of what is now accepted will later turn out to have been mistaken. Hence Polanyi criticises Bertrand Russell for his neglect of the role of authority in science. Russell had written [6]:

the principles of science are due to the substitution of observation and inference for authority. Every attempt to revive authority in intellectual matters is a retrograde step. And it is part of the scientific attitude that the pronouncements of science do not claim to be certain, but only the most probable on the basis of present evidence. One of the great benefits that science confers upon those who understand its spirit is that it enables them to live without the delusive support of subjective authority.

124

Polanyi comments [7]:

> Such statements obscure the fact that the authority of
> current scientific opinion is indispensable to the discipline
> of scientific institutions; that its functions are invaluable,
> even though its dangers are an increasing menace to
> scientific progress. I have seen no evidence that this
> authority is exercised without the claims of certainty for
> its own teachings. In any case it is a mistake to assume that
> it is easier to justify a scientific opinion that merely makes
> claims of probability than one that makes claims of
> certainty. Both express a commitment, and to this extent
> both must go beyond the evidence.

In the case of moral and political systems and of world-views
there is an equal or even greater need to maintain consistency
of attitude, although (and indeed because) this is more
difficult to do. Unlike the existing corpus of physical theory
they are in competition with a number of contemporary
rivals and each is normally subject to divergent interpretations on the part of those who subscribe to it. A textbook which claims to set out the theory of liberal democracy is thus doubly controversial. Hence W B. Gallie has
characterised the concepts employed by such theories as
'essentially-contested' [8]. The same is obviously true of
religious systems. Not only are all such systems incapable of
precise definition, but the comparatively imprecise defini-
tions that are put forward do not win universal acceptance.
Yet, as we have seen, they involve, to a much greater extent
than the sciences, the entire personalities of their adherents,
since it is among their chief functions to teach men how to
live. The principles of liberal democracy can flourish only in
a community in which men have learnt to think and act as
liberal democrats. They operate, that is to say, in the manner
of what Burke called 'prejudice with the reason involved' as
distinct from 'the naked reason' alone,

> ... because prejudice with its reason, has a motive to give
> action to that reason, and an affection that will give it
> permanence. Prejudice is of ready application in the

125

emergency; it previously engages the mind in a steady course of wisdom and virtue, and does not leave the man hesitating in the moment of decision, sceptical, puzzled and unresolved. Prejudice renders a man's virtue his habit; and not a series of unconnected acts. Through just prejudice his duty becomes part of his nature [9]

Burke does not use the word 'prejudice' in such a way as to imply that prejudices do not require or admit of rational justification — he speaks of 'prejudice with the reason involved' and 'just prejudice' — but he recognises that a man cannot develop any intellectual or moral depth and consistency if he is 'carried about with every wind of doctrine'. He casts doubt on the ideal of the wholly autonomous individual, perpetually subjecting all beliefs to criticism, and retaining at any time only those that at that time he is able to vindicate against all comers. This ideal, is impossible of realisation because every individual grows to maturity in a cultural tradition and remains to some extent dependent on that tradition for the terms in which he conceives his problems. Even in a plural society, in which opposing traditions are represented, he must, if he is to avoid superficiality, to some extent identify himself with one or other of them. If it is true, as has been argued earlier, that, outside of the natural sciences, the capacity to exercise sensitive and informed judgement depends upon and develops along with the acquisition of appropriate intellectual, moral and spiritual virtues, this provides a further reason why the individual must identify himself more fully with his beliefs than is suggested by the word 'hypothesis' [10].

It may still be objected that, however understandable it is, and however socially desirable it may be, that individuals should in this way identify themselves with such large-scale systems of belief, it is nevertheless not rational for them to do so. It is not enough for there to be reasons, to which appeal could be made; the individual must have reasons, which *ex hypothesi* he has not — at least to the extent necessary to justify the degree of confidence he manifests.

The way, in principle, to meet this objection would seem

126

to be on the lines adopted by Polanyi in connection with the attitude of the scientist. The argument there was that confident belief in the reliability of the existing corpus of scientific knowledge is a necessary condition of the individual's making effective criticisms of it or original contributions to it. Might not the same be said about other, non-scientific, systems of belief? To this it might be objected that it is simply not the case that such non-scientific systems are as firmly based as science is. Indeed it has already been admitted that their concepts are comparatively loosely defined and infected with controversy, both in the sense that those who accept a system differ as to its proper interpretation and in the sense that there are men of undoubted rationality who do not accept the system at all. Hence it cannot be right for a man to yield to such a system the sort of unhesitating assent which he does to a scientific system.

Nevertheless, is it not as true in the political case as in the scientific, that such assent is necessary if any progress is to be made in practice and in theory — bearing in mind the fact that in such matters practice and theory are interdependent? If it is the case, as surely it is, that any but the most primitive society requires a complex structure of institutions in order to enable its members to achieve certain shared purposes, and that this is a condition of their being able to achieve a variety of individual purposes, there has to be some, at least tacit, agreement as to the nature of these institutions and as to the purposes which they shall fulfil. The researches of sociologists and social anthropologists reveal that the actual and potential variety of possible institutions and their associated purposes is enormous; and, as was suggested earlier, to articulate the assumptions about human nature underlying different ways of solving the problems of a complex society is a task of great difficulty; yet it would certainly seem that there always are such assumptions and that it is desirable that they should be subject to critical appraisal. It is characteristic, for example, of liberal democracy that it sets a high value on the individual's freedom to think and speak freely although, notoriously, for the system to be able to work, a certain

127

restraint is demanded. And it appears likely that some shared values are necessary over and above those that define the liberal democratic system itself. Normally an area of political controversy exists in which contrasting social ideals are canvassed by different political parties, which themselves have their own, more or less completely worked out, theoretical principles. Within these there arise the same problems of the rationality of commitment.

Related to these shared systems of belief is the individual's own working 'philosophy of life', which may be more or less reflective and highly integrated, more or less original. The situation which does not and could not obtain is one in which the individual thought up his own philosophy of life entirely from scratch (although some educational theorists come near to supposing that this is or ought to be the case). As has already been argued, if such a situation were *per impossibile* to occur, there would be no regulated society and no cultural tradition; so that the individual would lack the linguistic and other intellectual resources that he needed, or the security in which to develop them if he had them. There could be no progress in the theory or the practice of politics (or of any other aspect of culture), unless the underlying principles were able to be tested over a sufficient period by groups of people who believed in them enough to make them work effectively.

Mention has been made of educational theory, and the problem of the relation between rationality and commitment can be seen as exemplified in the attitude of educational theorists to the educational 'philosophy' which they embrace. The most superficial acquaintance with the literature of the philosophy of education reveals that this is a matter about which views are strongly held. These views tend to range along a spectrum from extreme liberalism to extreme authoritarianism and to be associated with the individual's beliefs about the nature and potentialities of human beings and the way in which they should live in society. This is not surprising, since such views are bound to affect one's conception of the nature and purpose of education. For this

128

reason it is impossible to be neutral about them in educational practice. The educator may, indeed, be unreflective about them, but it is not difficult for the perceptive observer to discern the principles which in fact underlie his educational practice, and if challenged, he is bound to acknowledge or repudiate them.

The fact that these educational theories are controversial can scarcely be gainsaid. The progressive educationalist is bound to admit that there exist men of undoubted rationality and experience who do not accept the principles of progressive education and are, indeed, resolutely opposed to them. Similarly, the defender of traditional aims and methods must recognise that they are under attack from men who, by any standards, are educated and intelligent. It is simply not the case that the progressives or the traditionalists are in a position to show that their opponents have not the remotest chance of being right. This does not, however, weaken the conviction of both parties in their own rightness, and in the wrong-headedness of their opponents. Although, or perhaps because, the whole future character of the young is at stake, either party, given the opportunity, will mould the educational process in accordance with its ideals, using legal and institutional pressures without hesitation, where these are thought to be necessary.

It is easy for the detached onlooker to view this scene with a certain wry amusement, more especially as some of the protagonists regard themselves as models of toleration; and it is true that the latter often have less insight into their situation than they suppose. Nevertheless their situation is one in which a high degree of commitment is called for and detachment would be a dereliction of duty. Unless it does not matter how the young are educated (and this too would require to be substantiated) their education must be in accordance with some principles and not others, aimed at some ends and not others; and what these aims and principles should be is bound to be of serious concern. It may be that a sensible educator should avoid both extremes, but at whatever point he believes the correct balance should be struck, he must be ready, if he is to be successful, to commit himself

129

to the working out of the chosen policy with as much energy and enthusiasm as the extremists.

The problem of the authoritarian educator is less complex than that of the liberal. He knows what results he wants to achieve and his problems are set him only by the resistance of the human material. The liberal, however, is liable to find that he cannot, throughout the educational process, refrain altogether from imparting any bias to children that he is not able to justify to them on rational grounds. He cannot even be sure that a consistent policy of producing rational justifications whenever possible will be more effective in helping the child to become a rational adult than a somewhat more authoritarian approach would be. And this difficulty is associated with a certain incoherence in the extreme liberal's conception of what it is to be a rational adult. As I have been concerned to argue, a man who is prepared to change his mind about any of his beliefs whenever it appears to him that the evidence tells against them will not be able to hold on to them long enough to work them out and test them properly. If they are fundamental beliefs of a kind that have important moral and other implications for practice, he will never be able to follow out these implications or develop a serious and stable moral character. Both for his intellectual and his moral development it would seem to be necessary that a certain consistency of direction should be preserved from which the individual does not allow himself to deviate too readily. In the absence of this there occurs the special sort of silliness and subservience to fashion to which intellectuals are peculiarly susceptible.

When we speak of someone believing in a system of thought of some kind, we imply, as H. H. Price has pointed out [11], that he relies on it, in the expectation that it will help to render some area of experience more intelligible; if it is a metaphysical system, that it will help to render the world as a whole more intelligible. Such reliance is consistent with the recognition that the system is in some respects incomplete or inadequate or even that it contains contradictions, which are given the status of paradoxes. Our argument suggests that in relation to such systems, there are at least two reasons why reliance cannot be purely intellectual. One is that what the system is relied on for is guidance as to the way in which a man should live, that is to say what sort of man he should be. And living in that way, becoming that sort of man demands consistency of purpose, the continuous exercise of those virtues it is hoped to develop. The other is that, as Price also suggests, it is sometimes a necessary condition of a man's coming to appreciate certain truths (or what are regarded in the system as truths) that he should have acquired a suitable sort of character. As Price puts it: 'The latent assumption which needs to be made explicit is this: that a person's character, the conative and emotional dispositions he has acquired, affects his *cognitive* powers and enables him to be aware of facts he could not otherwise be aware of' [12]. Price makes this point in a religious context, but it may be applied more generally, for example, to ethics, as can most readily be seen in connection with the professional ethics of, say, a doctor. There are certain values to which, as a doctor, he is committed and his becoming a good doctor involves his cultivating those conative and emotional dispositions which are summed up in the expression 'tender loving care'; and his acquiring of these dispositions is, in turn, a necessary condition of his being able to make the ethical discriminations which his role requires of him. In the process he becomes a certain sort of man and it is men of this sort we need to have as doctors. One does not want hide-bound doctors, unable to respond to the ethical demands of novel situations, but the way to avoid this is not to refrain from inducting them into a strong professional tradition, but so to induct them into to it as to ensure that they do not emerge with closed minds and restricted sympathies. And for this to be possible it is important that the tradition should itself be a reasonable one.

Few philosophers have understood this process better than Aristotle, who insisted on the need for men to become habituated to a desirable pattern of feeling and acting as a necessary condition of their coming to understand its rational basis. What he did not realise was the extent to which ethical

131

systems are liable to be controversial. Recognition of this fact does not, however, affect the truth of his analysis of the relation between character and discernment in morality. The man who does not believe in anything with sufficient seriousness and consistency to test it in his life may make no mistakes; but he will not learn any lessons.

Implicit in what has been said, and complicating it still further, is the fact that people who subscribe to a particular system of belief vary very greatly in the degree of their understanding of it, and the extent to which they can make their understanding articulate. Very few people of liberal democratic convictions are able to 'give an account' or 'provide a rationale' of their beliefs; and those who can rarely feel confident that they have done so in a fully satisfactory fashion. The articulate believer in democracy can generally recognise a practice as undemocratic, even though he is hard put to it to explain at all precisely why it is so. He is in fact, in the position of those who were questioned by Socrates and were not able 'to give an account' (*logon didonai*) [13]. He is in a state of 'right opinion' (*orthe doxa*). A more articulate believer is able to 'give an account' while aware that he falls short of complete comprehension. He is in a state of 'understanding' (*dianoia*); others, equally articulate, may differ from him in emphasis and, indeed, may be alive to features of democracy which he neglects. It is reasonable to suppose that it will be a less straightforward matter to show how the inarticulate believer can be rationally justified in his belief than with the more articulate.

A tough-minded critic might wish to maintain that not only do these people not have the same reasons for believing what they do; they do not even have the same beliefs. For a man can only properly be said to believe in what he himself takes liberal democracy to be; and what he takes it to be is what he says it is when closely questioned. Since what will emerge from this process of questioning is either a variety of rather sketchy and confused notions or a range of comparatively clear but more or less divergent beliefs, one has to conclude that the respondents do not believe in the same thing at all. It is argued, for example, that opinion polls

132

which, on the face of it, reveal that, say, 84 per cent of the population believe in God, are totally misleading since closer questioning shows that they differ widely as to what they understand by 'God'. This is one reason why it is often thought better to use the test of formal membership of a church or political party, or regular participation in certain practices such as religious worship or voting in elections, as indications of what someone believes in.

However, this way of dealing with the problem is, surely, too restrictive. Both the inarticulate individual and the articulate, in trying to express their beliefs as best they can, tend to think of themselves as endeavouring to 'get at' something which could be more clearly or more adequately formulated in such a way that, if they were presented with this formulation, now or at some future time, they would say, 'Yes; that is just what I meant'. Indeed this is our normal situation at a given time with respect to most of our beliefs, including those which we have at some time been able to articulate. Button-holed by Socrates, we cannot here and now give an account, but we know we were once able to do so and believe that we could do so again in the future or, at least, that we could recognise it when done for us by someone else.

It is characteristic, then, of the sort of large-scale system that we have been considering

(i) that at no time does any individual completely understand all its ramifications;

(ii) that some individuals understand some parts of it better than others do;

(iii) that the 'fit' between the comparatively inarticulate hunches of some and the confident explications of others provides a link which justifies the claim that what they believe is substantially the same;

(iv) that there are those who are able either explicitly or implicitly to appreciate the unity and coherence of the system.

It is not something equally apparent to all or fully apparent to anyone, yet, assuming that it does have a

133

rationale, individual believers are, in their own fashion and in varying degrees, aware of the content of what they believe and of the reasons for believing it [14].

In the light of the argument of this chapter it can be seen that world-views and other large-scale systems of belief share two features commonly associated with religion:

1. Conversion from one system to another is rarely effected by rational argument alone, as it involves the believer's entire personality and his whole way of perceiving and responding to the world. And, since there are always difficulties to be endured and intellectual doubts to be faced, there is need for the power to resist temptation in either of these forms, so as to ensure that the believer does not waver when he ought to stand firm. There is, that is to say, a need for faith in one straightforward sense of the word.

2. Since *ex hypothesi*, it is always possible that the considerations which appear as temptations to be resisted might, when properly understood, provide sufficient reasons for a fundamental change of standpoint, there is, in a recognisable form, a perpetual possibility of tension between faith and reason.

It remains to consider whether Christian faith is simply a special case of this kind of secular faith or whether it has distinctive features of its own.

8 Faith and Revelation

If it is true, as my argument has suggested, not only of systems of religious belief, but also of secular world-views and moral and political theories that they require and admit of rational justification, but are not, and ought not to be, accepted by their adherents in a merely tentative and provisional manner, the complaint that, by assimilating the religious case to these others, I have overlooked the committed character of religious belief, loses much of its force. No doubt the character of religious faith is in important respects different, but the resemblances should not be neglected.

It is characteristic of any such system that it is highly ramified, and that it is capable of further articulation and development. Moreover, no single individual can comprehend all of it, even to the extent that it has at present been worked out; no one can fully apprehend its intellectual structure or completely appropriate the attitudes that go with it. There are, therefore, great variations in the way individuals are related to it. Some have a more synoptic view than others; some have penetrated more deeply than others; there are differences of interpretation and emphasis as well as varying degrees of practical involvement. It is difficult even for theorists, whose approach is primarily intellectual, to identify and express all the considerations which in fact guide their thinking and acting at the deepest level of their personalities, and this is even more evidently true of the many more who are not given to formulating their ideas precisely. And in all cases it is safe to presume that there are some influences at work which are incompletely rational and might be repudiated if the individual were aware of them.

It is precisely their appreciation of this situation which leads some thinkers to the conclusion that it is not possible even in principle for a rational choice to be made between such systems, on the ground that such a choice would require the individual to become independent of all the influences that have made him the man he is. They are right in thinking that a man cannot become a human being with a determinate character and outlook unless he undergoes an education, both formal and informal, based on one or more cultural traditions; but wrong in supposing that his rationality is thereby inevitably threatened. It may indeed be threatened by exposure to a cultural tradition that is illiberal and inhumane; but in the absence of any cultural tradition it cannot develop at all. While it is of the utmost importance to recognise that rationality is a cultural product in the sense that a suitable cultural history is a necessary condition of its growth and maintenance, the moral to be drawn from this is not that cultures cannot be judged from a rational point of view, but that a culture that encourages rationality is to be vigorously sought and energetically preserved. It is this that makes the difference between Burke's 'prejudice with the reason involved' and simple prejudice. A system which has the character of simple prejudice is unable to respond creatively to criticism, or modify itself in the face of experience that is new and apparently recalcitrant; it cannot therefore develop and must progressively lose whatever capacity it had to provide a satisfactory interpretation of the world. It takes on the character of Lakatos's 'degenerating problem-shift' [1].

However, sensitivity to criticism carries with it the possibility in principle that criticisms might be encountered which were cumulatively fatal. And it is this possibility which, in relation to religious belief, has generated the present problem. For it implies that circumstances might arise in which, when every allowance has been made for the legitimate demands of 'prejudice', the individual ought to give up his present belief and adopt another. But religious belief requires unconditional commitment.

It is necessary, therefore, to consider whether religious faith, or at any rate the faith of traditional Christian theism, differs in any fundamental respect from the sort of secular faith we have been examining. But, before we do so, it is worth emphasising once again the extent to which problems which we tend to associate uniquely with religious belief arise also in a secular context; in particular those which have to do with the process of conversion and the tension between faith and reason. Conversion from liberal democracy to Marxism or from humanism to naturalism (to use examples given earlier) involves as radical a transformation as conversion to or from Christianity and is equally unlikely to occur as a result of a single argument or series of arguments; it involves, intellectually, a massive shift in the overall appreciation and assessment of an immense range of facts and experiences and, with this, a new pattern of feeling and acting. Given the complexity of the positions from which and to which the convert passes, it is impossible even for the most articulate to appreciate all that is involved, and it may be only much later, if at all, that on reflection he can distinguish the reasons that actually weighed with him. In many cases the process is only implicitly rational; in others, barely rational at all. Hence in actual practice it is often the case that, in the words of Alasdair MacIntyre, 'Belief cannot reason with unbelief: it can only preach to it' [2] (it being assumed that 'preaching' is addressed to the emotions and the will rather than to the intellect).

If MacIntyre's epigram represented the whole truth, the second problem — of the tension between faith and reason — would not arise. Yet it is a matter of common experience that it does arise, and in secular as well as religious contexts. Raziel Abelson is correctly reflecting ordinary usage when he remarks that 'the expression "faith that . . . " functions as a disclaimer of plausible evidence for (and sometimes even as an admission of strong evidence against) the proposition whose truth it asserts'; and it is natural to conclude with him: 'Consequently, any declaration of the form "I have faith that . . . " is contrary to reason' [3]. Thus if a man holds some proposition as an 'article of faith' we know that he is not going to treat it as a matter for everyday argument; and there is no need to draw on 'reserves of faith' in order to enable one to respond to a situation as any reasonable man

137

might in any case be expected to respond to it. The magnificence of Churchill's faith in ultimate victory in the summer of 1940 depends on the odds having been heavily against him.

Nevertheless it may still be objected that this familiar opposition between faith and reason presupposes that faith is not itself based on reasons. For if it were, there could be no conflict. The man of faith would persevere in his faith only so long as it remained on balance more likely than not that he would turn out to be right in the end. Only if he persisted beyond that point would it be proper to talk of a conflict between faith and reason.

This objection would stand if men could be supposed always to have full and explicit understanding of the rational basis of their beliefs and to be able to survey at any time the entire state of the question. But this, as we have seen, is rarely, if ever, the case. The individual does not see everything, nor can he always see clearly what he does see; nor is his judgement unaffected by confused emotions and uncertain purposes. It is in this characteristically human predicament that faith belongs. There would be no need for faith in a world where men had no tendency to lose heart and where circumstances were always clear, stable and unambiguous; and faith would not be a virtue unless it were both difficult and necessary for men to pursue a steady course in the face of dangers, doubts and frustrations. In this situation faith, even when it is in fact reasonable, must often operate in the individual's life as a substitute for reason rather than as a straightforward expression of it. And it must often appear to him that reason is at odds with it, the more especially as 'reason' is readily identified with what can be clearly stated and easily recognised or even with what is currently fashionable or commonly accepted.

It is not surprising, therefore, that it is those whose beliefs depend upon evidence that is not very palpable or tangible, requiring sensitivity and judgement for its recognition, who are most aware of this tension. Although the naturalist is no more in a position than the humanist to show beyond all reasonable doubt that he is right, and is therefore open to

138

temptation to abandon his naturalism if confronted with examples of profound human responses which cannot without strain be accommodated in his system, it is very much easier to ignore or neglect such evidence than it is for the humanist to divert his attention from the progress of cybernetics. In secular cases too, faith tends to be 'the substance of things hoped for, the evidence of things not seen'.

There is, then, a readily intelligible sense of 'faith' in which it is proper to talk of faith in secular and religious contexts without equivocation. And some of the problems associated with religious faith are problems that arise with faith in this sense. However nothing that we have said about this sort of faith could justify the claims commonly made on behalf of the Christian's faith in God that it is, and ought to be, a matter of unconditional commitment, since the possibility always remains that in the end the believer's entire system of thought might be undermined in such a manner that he could and should no longer adhere to it.

Yet these claims cannot be gainsaid. There is a sense in which Christian faith is unconditional. The only way out of the impasse is to conclude that the sense in which faith is unconditional is a different one, which is indeed peculiar to a theistic religion. This is the sense of 'faith' as 'trusting reliance upon God' ('fides' in the sense of 'fiducia'). The theist is bound to maintain his trust in God's goodness and mercy, no matter what dangers and difficulties confront him. So Job can say, 'Though he slay me, yet will I trust in him'. He is lacking in faith if he extends his trust only so far as the course of events seems to justify it. Faith, in this sense, is analogous to faith in a person, which is a necessary condition of any stable and profound personal relationship, and must go beyond the evidence that is ordinarily available to justify it. Like faith in another person, it presupposes the existence of its object. The most fervent monarchist would not insist on unconditional commitment to the present king of France, unless he believed that there still existed a rightful claimant to the throne. Thus, although there is a Christian duty to

139

trust in God, this does not imply a duty, let alone an unconditional duty, to go on believing that there is a God. Indeed, once it is admitted to be a genuine possibility that there is no God and that the case against his existence might become cumulatively overwhelming, it is pointless to maintain that one ought to go on believing nevertheless that there is a God, even when the belief could be seen to be false. It could not, in these circumstances be a duty owed to God, and there is no other conceivable reason why it should be a duty. This is to say that the requirement of unconditional faith is one which has its place within the system of theistic belief and cannot properly be interpreted as an obligation to continue to embrace the system itself.

Yet this way of dealing with the difficulty, although in principle correct, is perhaps too simple as it stands. The temptation to apostasy is really a temptation, and the fact that the believer's relation to God is a personal one gives it a somewhat different character from the kind of temptation that a man may experience to give up a purely secular faith. Just as it is sometimes a duty to believe in a man when appearances are against him, it is a duty to believe in God when the appearances are against him; and the human situation is such that the appearances are often against his existing at all. A faith which could not cope with this predicament would be of little value. There is a possible analogy to this in the parable of the Stranger which I put into circulation some time ago [4]. Given that it would be an obvious move against the partisans for the occupying power to put it about that the Stranger was dead, it might be incumbent on those who had faith in the Stranger not to be too ready to credit such reports. Indeed it is possible that something similar may be true also of certain sorts of secular faith. A Marxist may regard himself as unconditionally committed to the international working class. It is true that this commitment holds good only if there is such a thing as an international working class, as understood by Marxists, so that, if it became cumulatively evident that Marxism was false, he would be justified in repudiating it along with the entire Marxist system.

But the fact that, if there is indeed a mass of people dependent upon himself and others like him for liberation from an unjust class system, they have a serious claim upon him, is enough to make him less prepared than he would otherwise be to abandon his Marxism. If there is such a legitimate claim, he ought to respond to it; and, in order to respond to it, he must recognise it, and therefore take extra care not to be wrongly tempted away from his adherence to that conceptual system which enables him to recognise it if indeed it is there.

For this reason it is not possible to treat these two senses of 'faith' quite separately. It must affect a man's faith in Christianity as a world-view that failure to maintain it can be one way of failing in trusting reliance on God; and the believer cannot but recognise that his faith in God is bound up with his belief in Christianity. Nevertheless, when due allowance has been made for this, it is an error to assimilate faith in Christianity to faith in God and to credit the former with the unconditional character that belongs only to the latter. To do this is to remove the rational constraints which maintain the essential connection between the system of Christian belief and the many and various considerations upon which it rests. The arguments of theologians are then left without rational support and beyond reach of rational criticism. Bultmann, for example, achieves precisely this result when he writes [5]:

Our radical attempt to demythologize the New Testament is in fact a perfect parallel to St. Paul's and Luther's doctrine of justification by faith alone apart from the works of the Law. Or rather it carries this doctrine to its logical conclusion in the field of epistemology. Like the doctrine of justification it destroys every false demand for it on the part of man, whether he seeks it in his good works or in his ascertainable knowledge. The man who wishes to believe in God as his God must realize that he has nothing in his hand on which to base his faith.

There is not in point of fact any warrant in logic for
141

proceeding from the theological doctrine of justification by faith alone to the epistemological doctrine that faith admits of no rational support. The former insists that man cannot earn salvation by good works and is a part of the teaching of traditional Christian theism (which has received especial emphasis in the Lutheran tradition); the latter claims that traditional Christian theism, of which this theological doctrine is a part, must be accepted without question by an existential choice for which no reason can or need be given. They are entirely distinct and it is an evident *non sequitur* to suppose that the one follows from the other.

It was objected to my earlier account of the rational structure of traditional Christian theism that it implied that Christian faith ought to be tentative and provisional. I have endeavoured to answer this objection by pointing out (i) that there is an important sense of 'faith' in which it is true to say of Christian faith that it is unconditional, viz. the sense of 'faith' as trusting reliance on God, and (ii) that even in the sense of faith which is (with some qualifications) univocal in secular and religious contexts, that of faith in a world-view or other large-scale system of belief, it is by no means the case that men are or should be ready to give it up at all readily in the face of doubts and difficulties.

But this line of argument is likely to awaken further objections on the part of those who will be inclined to feel that my account has assimilated religious belief, or at any rate Christian belief, too completely to these other systems. In the end, it will be said, in spite of all the qualifications, theology has been reduced to a sort of metaphysics, a construction of the human mind to be judged, appropriately enough if that is what it is, by whatever criteria there are for assessing such constructions. But theology, if it deserves to be taken seriously at all, must be more than this; it must be, or in some way represent, a divine revelation and, as such, it cannot be amenable to the sort of rational test that would otherwise be in place. At an earlier stage in the discussion it was recognised that there might be peculiarities of the theological case which should prevent its being assimilated to the others, and this possibility must now be faced.

142

It is not entirely easy to do this, because theologians, in attempting to vindicate the immunity of theological claims from rational test, have often relied on theories of a relativistic kind, which are believed by them to hold quite generally. Hence they have not thought it necessary to distinguish at all carefully the particular features of a theological system which require it to be treated differently from the others It was for this reason, indeed, that I deliberately chose to consider these general theories first in their non-theological applications.

If our earlier argument is to be trusted, these theories will not bear the weight which theologians have wished to place on them. The objection we now have to consider is independent of them. It is stated concisely by Reinhold Niebuhr [6]:

> Religious faith cannot be simply subordinated to reason or made to stand under its judgement ... When this is done, the reason which asks the question whether the God of religious faith is plausible has already implied a negative answer to the question, because it has made itself God, and naturally cannot tolerate another.

Karl Barth, with whom this thesis is especially associated, states it as follows [7]:

> God's revelation has its reality and truth wholly and in every respect ... within itself. Only by denying it can we wish to ascribe to it a higher or deeper ground, different from itself, or regard, adopt or reject it from the standpoint of such a higher or deeper ground. Obviously the adoption of revelation from the vantage of such a ground, different from it and presumably superior to it, e.g. an affirmation of revelation in which a man previously set up his conscience to be a judge of it; can only be achieved by denying revelation.

In terms of what Barth and Niebuhr here say the objection to our previous account of the part played by revelation in a

143

cumulative case for traditional Christian theism must be that such an account accords revelation a merely subordinate role. It is left in the end to human judgement to determine whether words or events which purport to be revelatory are so or not and, if it decides they are, how they are to be interpreted. That there are (if there are) phenomena which appear to demand the status of revelations is, on that view, an argument of some force for the existence of a God who might reveal himself in such a manner, but it is an argument which cannot stand alone, but requires the support of reasons which are independent of the putative revelation. The idea that a divine revelation must necessarily enjoy an unchallengeable status has led some other thinkers to repudiate revelations altogether. Brand Blanshard writes in a criticism of Paul Tillich [8]:

> If God is really thus transcendent — transcendent of all the prescriptions of human reason in metaphysics and ethics — then any attempts by reason to construe his nature or his will must end in complete misconstruction . . . If God is 'wholly other', the attempt of rational men to lead reasonable lives is as little likely to represent his will as the life of some wayward beatnik or some dervish from Berchtesgaden.

Revelation, he argues, must be measured by reason, not reason by revelation. But then:

> What is the difference, after all, between one who takes reason as the guide of life and one who, accepting revelation as the guide, imposes the test of reason on the candidates to revelation?

Blanshard poses a dilemma: either revelation is totally immune from rational criticism, or it is subject to such criticism. If the former, it is wholly discontinuous with our ordinary standards of what is reasonable and right; if the latter, it can have no independent authority. This dilemma, in one form or another, has been enormously persuasive. The conclusions that it allows are neither of them capable of giving the theist much satisfaction. Yet he can scarcely be prepared to dispense with revelation, for, if there is any substance in theism at all, it would seem to require that men should depend for much, if not all, of their knowledge of God upon his own disclosure of his character and purposes. It is not surprising, therefore, that the concept of revelation is present in all the higher religions (with the obvious exception of Buddhism). There is an evident incoherence in the notion that God, as conceived in the Judaeo-Christian tradition, should create men in his own image with the intention that they should come to know and love him, and yet should in no way communicate with them. But it is more radically incoherent to suppose that God should indeed 'communicate' with men, but in a language wholly discontinuous with that which they ordinarily speak.

The unsatisfactoriness of these alternatives is enough to cast doubt on the assumptions underlying the dilemma. The basic assumption would seem to be that once it is conceded that rational tests of any kind may properly be applied to a putative revelation, the revelation itself, even if it succeeds in passing the tests, is thereby deprived of any independent authority. So that if the traditional Christian theist is rationally persuaded that God revealed himself in the life and death of Jesus Christ and in his teaching, and if he applies his powers of reasoning to the problem of interpreting that revelation, he has in effect substituted his own judgement for the word of God. And this is tantamount to saying that reason can be in a position to judge a claim to revelation only if reason could in principle, without the aid of revelation, discover that which is supposed to be revealed.

The oddness of this assumption emerges clearly if one develops the analogy upon which the notion of divine revelation depends: that of another person's communicating to me intentions and purposes which I could not discover unless he chose to tell me. If there is a reason to doubt whether he is the person he purports to be, I am not obliged to believe him until I have satisfied myself upon the point. I can and should use my critical judgement in order to tell whether he is deceiving me. I may and should rely on his manner and expression and my antecedent knowledge of his character to determine how serious and sincere he is; and I may be wise to check his statements by his subsequent behaviour. Yet, however careful my scrutiny, I cannot discover entirely on my own what he alone is able to tell me. If we apply the dilemma to this familiar situation we see at once that it poses false alternatives. There are, of course, important differences between this simple case and the position of the religious believer in relation to what he takes to be divine revelation, but they are not sufficient to undercut the analogy.

It is probable that the dilemma would not have proved so attractive if its proponents had not relied on some of the considerations we examined earlier. The language of Barth and Niebuhr is remarkably reminiscent of Kuhn's, and their distrust of reason seems largely to depend on an assumption, which they share with Kuhn, about the way in which reason operates. They appear to take it for granted that, if reason is brought to bear upon a putative revelation, this must consist in the application of a set of ready-made criteria. Since these criteria will have been the product of some already existing system of thought which, *ex hypothesi*, will not have been influenced by the revelation, to judge the revelation in terms of them will be to beg the question against it. Either, then, the revelation will be rejected or, as a condition of acceptance, it will be interpreted so as to conform entirely with the existing system of thought. Precisely similar reasoning persuades Kuhn that the transition from one scientific paradigm to another cannot be a rational one.

If Barth is assuming that in order to judge the genuineness of a claim to revelation we should have to be fully equipped in advance with a complete set of standards by which to judge it, he is right to regard this as preposterous. How could we know in advance of God's self-disclosure just what form such a disclosure must take? And if we did, what need would there be of revelation? As a protest against any such notion one can see the point of Barth's insistence that 'God's revelation has its reality and truth wholly and in every respect within itself'. Yet, in denying that we can have any grounds for accepting a claim to revelation, he is simply embracing an unwarranted paradox, as can be seen from our habit, in colloquial English, of using the word 'revelation' in talking about some outstanding exponent of an art — 'Menuhin's rendering was a revelation of the possibilities of the instrument'. What, presumably, we mean is that he makes us aware of possibilities which we could not ourselves have anticipated. If our judgement upon Menuhin's performance presupposed that we were in a position (before listening to him) to specify, in any but the most general terms, the qualities it must have in order to gain our amazed approbation, then, as admirers of it, we should feel obliged to take up a Barthian position and deny that we can assess it at all from 'a ground differing from it and presumably superior to it'. All the same we would not want to regard our preference for Menuhin over merely competent performers as an arbitrary and uninformed 'leap of faith'.

What this example illustrates is the unprofitability of approaching any instance of supreme creativity with a set of ready-made criteria. One of the marks of genuine originality in any field is precisely its capacity to surprise us and impose upon us its own standards. It is the minor artists of any age who conform most closely to the contemporary canons of style or good taste. And yet, as T. S. Eliot points out, the work of the great innovators is seen in retrospect to be not wholly discontinuous with what went before. We should make nothing of it if this were so, or if it had no power to illuminate our experience and understanding.

If this is true of human creativity, it is true *a fortiori* of divine revelation. Austin Farrer remarks [9]:

> In most fields of inquiry it is possible to set up models of argument and canons of proof. The usefulness of such aids varies greatly from one field to another. In the matter of revelation it must surely reach a vanishing point. If there is no *a priori* model for the form of God's self-disclosure, how can there be *a priori* canons for the marks of its authenticity?

In this he is almost echoing Bishop Butler: 'We cannot lay down *a priori* the method, the measure or the meaning of Revelation'. But it does not in the least follow from this that our total response to such a revelation cannot be a rational one. Indeed it is as true of theology as of any other system of thought that, unless its practitioners are prepared to recognise and accommodate any evidence that can be shown to be relevant, it cannot grow or even maintain itself as a coherent system.

If Barthians have been led to choose one of the false alternatives mentioned earlier, liberal theologians have often been tempted by the other. Identifying 'reason' with some secular system of thought, they have tended to accept only so much of traditional Christian theism as they believe to be consistent with 'reason' so understood; the rest being rejected or reinterpreted. In this way they substitute an uncritical acceptance of prevailing secular orthodoxies for an uncritical acceptance of traditional Christianity. It may, of course, be the case that their conclusions are correct, but the question cannot be decided without a careful and critical consideration of all the claims involved.

The foregoing discussion about the status and credentials of revelation as understood in traditional Christian theism has been somewhat abstract and jejune. An attempt must now be made, however briefly, to bring it into relation with the actual business of theologians and biblical scholars.

It is the claim of traditional Christianity that God has revealed himself in certain historical happenings, above all in the life and death of Jesus Christ. To constitute a revelation it is necessary not only that certain events should occur, but that they should rightly be interpreted as a disclosure of God's purposes. Hence it has also been claimed that the prophetic and apostolic witness to the events is inspired by God. Revelation then, to use William Temple's expression, involves 'the coincidence of event and interpretation. God guides the process, He guides the minds of men; the interaction of the process and the minds which are alike guided by Him is the essence of revelation' [10]. Comment-

148

ing on Temple's words, John Baillie writes [11]:

> This means that the gracious action of God is behind the response men make to His approach, as well as in the approach itself; and this has been the constant testimony of those who have in fact responded. The prophets and apostles all believed that only by God's own aid were they enabled to interpret His mighty acts. 'Surely', says Amos, 'the Lord God will do nothing but he revealeth his secrets unto his servants the prophets'.

It is obvious that this view of the matter itself involves a good deal of interpretation. Purely secular thinkers would reject it altogether and many contemporary theologians would find it in various ways unsatisfactory. It is impossible to explore all the problems which it raises. Fortunately, for my present purpose it is not necessary to do more than indicate the sort of argument that has to take place. The argument must centre on the treatment of certain historical documents, chiefly those which comprise the New Testament, because it is upon these documents that we must rely for our knowledge of the events which are claimed to be revelatory, and it is the writers of these documents — or at any rate some of them — who are said to have been inspired to interpret the events as constituting a divine self-disclosure. Our dependence on the documents immediately entails that the findings of various types of empirical inquiry are relevant. The work of historians, archaeologists, biblical critics, linguistic scholars has a bearing on the understanding of this material, and has to be taken into account, if the theological doctrines based upon it are not to be deprived of their foundations.

It may be objected that this form of words is question-begging and fails to take account of the role of theological presuppositions in interpreting the material. It is true that these are important, as will subsequently become clear, but it is no use importing presuppositions which are plainly incompatible with the available evidence or can be accommodated to it only by devices that are forced or fantastic. To take an extreme case, if good historical evidence were to

149

accumulate tending strongly to show that the gospels were forgeries and that Jesus was a fictitious character, there must come a point at which it would no longer be possible to accept the doctrine of the Incarnation, and this conclusion could not then be resisted by the claim that belief in the Incarnation is for Christians a presupposition of historical inquiry. It would not do, either, to appeal to a concept of 'sacred history' as providing a warrant for beliefs about the past which are entirely independent of the investigations of ordinary historians; for, if such a sacred history indeed refers to the past, and it conflicts with the findings of historical inquiry, its truth can only be maintained at the cost of repudiating in principle the ordinary historian's ways of finding out about the past. And this is an incoherent policy because these are the means we do and must employ throughout our everyday lives.

It is possible to approach the material with presuppositions of an entirely naturalistic or humanistic kind. Such an approach may be equally dogmatic, though less absurdly so, since the principles it relies on have some independent support. It is favoured not only by atheists but increasingly by theologians of a radical temper. They assume that the events in question are capable of being understood in purely natural terms and claim that, unless this is so, we can have no warrant for supposing that they occurred. The notion of God's acting in history, as traditionally understood, is therefore automatically excluded and with it the divine inspiration of biblical writers, which would itself have to be a special case of this divine activity. Appeal is often made to the outlook of modern man who, in Bultmann's words, is unable to countenance interference with 'the closed web of cause and effect'. In other words a scientific world-view is presupposed which is often thought to carry the authority of natural science. We have already seen, however, that like other world-views, it is in fact controversial. The success of natural science undoubtedly lends it some support, but it is very far from being established beyond reasonable doubt. The whole tenor of our earlier discussion should make it clear that the historian or biblical critic is fully entitled to operate

150

with this assumption, so long as he is prepared to realise that it is an assumption which stands in need of rational defence. By the same token the traditional Christian theist is entitled to challenge it, so long as he too realises that it is incumbent upon him to justify his own position. In attempting to do so, as we have seen, he will need to show that a theistic interpretation makes better overall sense than the alternatives. He clearly has no hope of doing this if it is stipulated in advance that, in assessing the documentary evidence, no allowance may be made for the possible activity of God, for his case will have to be that there are independent grounds for belief in God; that God would not leave his creatures without recourse; and that here, if anywhere, is an inspired record of a life and death through which God acted for men's salvation.

It is sometimes argued, following Hume, that the nature of 'scientific history' is such that it cannot give any support to the theist's case, not on the dogmatic ground criticised earlier that there can be no divine acts which interfere with 'the closed web of cause and effect', but on the more modest ground that 'scientific history' must proceed on naturalistic assumptions. This being so, it is contended, there must be an unbridgeable gap between the findings of 'scientific history' and the claims of the theologian of a kind which renders impossible the sort of cumulative case upon which the theist has to rely. This argument appears not to succeed, even if we set aside the disagreement that might occur between a liberal and a Marxist historian as to the nature of scientific history. It suffers from a serious ambiguity. It is one thing to say that a scientific historian may not offer other than naturalistic explanations — he may not, for example, be other than neutral as to what happened to St Paul on the road to Damascus. It is another thing to say that he must, *qua* scientific historian, provide a complete naturalistic explanation of St Paul's experience in terms, say, of abnormal psychology. He may, of course, do this if, as it happens, the evidence is clear enough to justify it, but he is not failing in his duty as a scholar if he concludes simply that Paul had an experience of a dramatic kind which altered the whole tenor

151

of his life and which he took to be an encounter with the risen Lord. Similarly with the more problematic case of the Resurrection itself. If there were, as in principle there might be, evidence to justify an entirely straightforward naturalistic explanation of what occurred, the scientific historian must, of course, accept it; but if there is not, he is under no obligation to adopt the most plausible naturalistic explanation on offer in order to leave no gaps in 'the closed web of cause and effect'. Given the controversial nature of religious claims and the known practical difficulties of securing agreement about them, it is a wise policy for the historian not to pronounce upon them; but he is not bound to rule against them. It is another question, and in its own context an entirely proper one, whether in the light of what historical inquiry discovers a religious or a purely naturalistic interpretation of what happened is to be preferred. The question cannot be considered in isolation from the more general question of the over-all adequacy of the rival systems of thought; nor can that question fail to turn in some degree upon the findings of historical inquiry in this and similar cases.

Temple wrote 'God guides the process. He guides the minds of men', and it is part of traditional Christian theism to claim that in some sense the Bible was divinely inspired. The whole subject of inspiration has been bedevilled by crude doctrines of verbal inerrancy and the like, and the very natural reaction against them. Critical methods have revealed the variety of standpoints to be found among the biblical writers and the complexity of influences upon them, to the extent that many theologians are persuaded that the Bible is to be regarded as neither more nor less authoritative than any other set of writings. It is, of course, possible 'that they are right to come to this conclusion; but it is important that it should be arrived at only after an exhaustive examination of the possible alternatives and not as a consequence of uncriticised philosophical assumptions. At an earlier stage I suggested that the basic analogy underlying the concept of revelation was a person's disclosure of his own intentions and purposes. I admitted at the time that this was too simple and required a number of qualifications. The most obvious of
152

these is that when God 'speaks' he does not do so directly, but through the words of men who, like all men, have become what they are through particular cultural influences and have their individual cast of thought. If one looks for an analogy to this situation, the most appropriate one seems to be that of the relation between a teacher and his pupils. Since the pupils vary in ability, temperament and interests, the teacher's influence will show itself in varying degrees and in a fragmentary fashion. Some of them will understand him better than others and they will differ from each other in emphasis and scope. Other influences, besides that of the teacher, will be present and discernible. Yet it is not impossible to discover what his teachings must have been. It is true that God does not literally speak or write or use the other devices by which teachers communicate with their pupils, and that we cannot, in the case of divine inspiration, identify the teacher independently of the pupils. We can, therefore, raise the question whether there is any 'teacher'. Why not, more economically, attribute all the ideas to the pupils themselves who together constitute a new movement? Originality is, after all, a human characteristic.

However, there is a partial analogy to this in the case where we cannot actually identify a teacher independently of the pupils. We may yet have good reason to postulate his existence and the character of his influence. One reason would be the testimony of the pupils themselves. That some of them acknowledged his influence would be comparatively strong evidence; that others, who also seemed to betray it, did not, would not do much to weaken this evidence (though it would if they denied it). Another indication would be the observed difference between what the pupils achieve when they have (as they claim) come under the teacher's influence and what they achieved before.

There are two further problems upon which the analogy does, I suggest, throw some light.

(i) The first is the relation between divine inspiration and human thought. It is sometimes argued that the human author must either be a passive agent (which raises all the problems of inerrancy as well as being psychologically implausible and plainly inapplicable to many of the biblical

153

writers) or be employing his own creative capacities to the full (leaving no room for the alleged activity of God). If the teacher-pupil analogy is invoked here, it serves to remind us that the most successful teacher is one who enables the pupil so to stretch his own intellectual powers as to grasp what he otherwise could not. How this is done is among the mysteries of the art, but it is certainly incompatible with the pupil's remaining passive. In so far as the teacher is successful, it becomes impossible to apportion the responsibility between teacher and pupil; it was necessary that each should make a full contribution. In so far as he is unsuccessful, the pupil will employ the familiar prefatory formula, 'the errors are my own'.

(ii) Very tentatively, it may be possible to develop this aspect of the analogy to the point of illuminating the Incarnation itself. A pupil who displayed striking originality while at the same time insisting upon his complete dependence upon a teacher would, if he were taken seriously, be regarded as of one mind with his teacher.

Even if, with the help of some such analogy, we can meet some of the difficulties attaching to the notion of divine inspiration, there are at least two other awkward problems.

(a) The first is put concisely by Dennis Nineham [12]:

It might appear that in order to have any basis for judging how far the unsuitable thought-forms and the inevitable human limitation . . . of the original recipients distorted or obscured the revelation, he (the modern interpreter) would need independent access to the revelation, which *ex hypothesi* he cannot have.

It would be absurd to try to deal with this problem in a page or two, but it is worth noticing that the appearance of a total logical impasse is misleading. Where the intentions of one person are communicated to others who in some respects obscure or distort them, it is not the case that the only way to correct the errors is by direct access to the original speaker. There are other tests of consistency, coherence and probability which can enable a critical and perceptive

154

judgement. Otherwise the task of critical exegesis would be impossible. In the theological case the task is dauntingly complex and beyond any individual's unaided resources, which is one reason why emphasis upon the Church is justified.

(b) The second problem might be put as follows: if, as is conceded, the divine inspiration of the Bible is no guarantee of infallibility, and supposing that the Church is able to check in some degree the inadequacies of the biblical writers, what is gained by supposing them divinely inspired and not simply inspired? Would not their value for us and their authority for us be the same? To put this in another way; what is the difference between the authority of someone who we have reason to believe is in certain respects wiser than we are, and someone who we have reason to believe is divinely inspired, if in each case we have to rely in the end on our own (individual or corporate) judgement as to the limits of his greater wisdom or his divine inspiration? If there is no difference, then, as indicated earlier, economy tells in favour of the simpler hypothesis.

The answer, I think, must be that it depends on the content of what is disclosed. Perhaps the teacher-pupil relationship may once again be invoked. If what we are interested in, and what the pupils claim to derive from the teacher, is certain truths which he is said to have discovered, but which anyone in principle might have discovered, we lose nothing (other things being equal) by eliminating the teacher and attributing them to the pupils. If, however, we are concerned with truths which could have been known only to the teacher (e.g., about his own intentions and purposes), the case is obviously altered. Even the derived and edited reports of the pupils have an authority which their own first-hand speculations could not have. Revelation has traditionally been conceived on the latter analogy. It will be seen that the theist's argument moves in a kind of spiral. Stage 1 consists in establishing or rendering plausible the claim that there is to be found in the work of biblical writers a total position which is important, consistent and distinctive and which, therefore, demands to be taken seriously. Stage 2 consists in

155

identifying and clarifying this position, which is found to involve certain claims about the nature and activity of God. Stage 3 evaluates these claims: are they (*a*) to be rejected as unintelligible or false? (*b*) to be accepted at their face value? (*c*) to be accepted in a modified form? Among these claims, arguably, is that the Bible itself contains a revelation of God in the sense that it records events of decisive religious significance witnessed and reflected upon by men who were able under the guidance of the Holy Spirit to grasp that significance. If this claim is accepted, then, Stage 4, the way is open to a fully developed dogmatic theology in which the Bible is treated as authoritative.

If this, or something like it, is the process by which traditional Christian theism requires to be justified, it is clear that there can be no question of evading critical questions by direct appeal to biblical or other dogmatic authority. A case has first to be made out for the entire system of thought in terms of which alone such an appeal is intelligible. On the other hand, if it can be made out — and it is not the purpose of this book to say whether it can or not — what will, *ex hypothesi*, have been shown or rendered plausible is that there are truths which men could not have discovered by themselves, but which God has found means of communicating to them. This does not imply that there is no room for further understanding or development, nor that it is possible to prescribe in advance the limits of interpretation. Since the biblical writers were fallible human beings whose knowledge was in many ways enormously inferior to our own, it will be necessary from time to time to re-draw the boundaries of their authority. In so doing we are bound to employ all the evidence and all the powers of reasoning that we have at our command, and the task will always be complex and exacting. If there is a divine revelation, it cannot be supposed that the task of understanding it will be less arduous, less demanding of all our faculties, less impossible of final completion than that of interpreting a human author.

156

Notes

INTRODUCTION

1. As 'traditional Christian theism' is a rather clumsy expression I shall sometimes talk instead of 'theism' or 'Christianity'.

CHAPTER 1

1. See Kai Nielsen, 'Contemporary Critiques of Religion', for discussion and bibliography.
2. Ibid., p. 116 ff.
3. See R. G. Swinburne, 'The Concept of Miracle', p. 56. I have also been helped by Mr M. R. McLean's doctoral thesis, 'The Idea of a Transcendent God'.
4. J. N. Findlay, 'Can God's Existence be Disproved?' in 'New Essays in Philosophical Theology', ed. Flew and MacIntyre.
5. See especially Terence Penelhum, 'Divine Necessity' in 'Mind' (1960); reprinted in 'The Philosophy of Religion', ed. Basil Mitchell. Penelhum does not take his argument to show the non-existence of God, but only of a God who is thought of as self-explanatory.
6. pp. 21–3.
7. See 'Hume on Evil' in 'God and Evil', ed. Nelson Pike, for a fuller discussion of this point.
8. See, e.g., Antony Flew, 'Divine Omnipotence and Human Freedom' in 'New Essays in Philosophical Theology', ed. Flew and MacIntyre; D. Z. Phillips, 'Death and Immortality'; J. L. Mackie, 'Evil and Omnipotence'; Alvin Plantinga, 'The Free Will Defence', both reprinted in 'The Philosophy of Religion', ed. Basil Mitchell. For a selected bibliography, see 'God and Evil', ed. Nelson Pike.
9. Op. cit., especially chs. 2–4.
10. Ibid., p. 59.
11. That it is not has been plausibly argued by G. B. Matthews, 'Theology and Natural Theology' in 'Journal of Philosophy' (1964).

12. In 'Theology and Verification' in 'Theology Today' (1962); reprinted in 'The Philosophy of Religion', ed. Basil Mitchell. Also 'Faith and Knowledge', p. 186 ff.

13. Op. cit., p. 187.

14. Op. cit., p. 77.

15. Ibid., p. 78.

16. Ibid., pp. 33—5.

17. See 'Philosophy and Language' in 'The Concept of a Person and other Essays', p. 21.

18. Nielsen, op. cit., pp. 45-54.

19. Ibid., p. 52.

20. See, for example, R. C. Zaehner, 'Mysticism Sacred and Profane'; Ninian Smart, 'Philosophers and Religious Truth' and 'Doctrine and Argument in Indian Philosophy'; W. T. Stace, 'Mysticism and Philosophy'.

21. See especially ch. 5.

22. 'Identification and Existence' in 'Contemporary British Philosophy', 3rd series, ed. H. D. Lewis.

23. Nielsen, op. cit., pp. 37—40.

24. Ibid., p. 37.

25. See ch. 6 of the present work.

CHAPTER 2

1. The sense of 'probable' involved here is that in which the probability of an event is determined by its relation to a class or classes of similar events. Hick remarks, '. . . If the event in question — in this case the recurrence of the universe — is so defined that there can be no other events, then the notion of probability cannot be brought to bear upon it.' 'Arguments for the Existence of God', p. 28.

2. 'Anselm's Ontological Arguments' in 'Philosophical Review' (1960); reprinted in 'The Many-Faced Argument', ed. Hick and McGill.

3. Findlay, op. cit.

4. 'Meditations', V, trans. Haldane and Ross, 'The Philosophical Works of Descartes', I, p. 182.

5. 'Critique of Pure Reason', trans. Kemp Smith, p. 505.

6. Notably by Jerome Shaffer, 'Existence, Predication and the Ontological Argument' in 'Mind' (1962); reprinted in 'The Many-Faced Argument', ed. Hick and McGill. See also Jonathan Barnes, 'The Ontological Argument', ch. 3.

7. 'Arguments for the Existence of God', p. 83.

8. Op. cit., p. 306.

9. Shaffer, op. cit., p. 245.

10. Malcolm, op. cit., pp. 306—7.

11. See Antony Flew, 'God and Philosophy', chs. 3—5. For difficulties in the idea of a self-explanatory being see Terence Penelhum, 'Divine Necessity' in 'Mind' (1960); reprinted in 'The Philosophy of Religion', ed. Basil Mitchell.

12. Cf. Ninian Smart, 'Philosophers and Religious Truth', p. 83 ff.

13. Hick, op. cit., p. 51.

14. 'God and Philosophy', p. 69.

15. See ch. 1, p. 19f.

16. Cf. R. G. Swinburne, 'The Concept of Miracle', ch. 5. I should also like to express indebtedness to an unpublished paper by Mr M. R. McLean.

17. Austin Farrer, 'The Freedom of the the Will', p. 58.

18. Smart, op. cit., p. 97.

19. Ibid., p. 97.

20. Flew, op. cit., p. 74.

21. Hick, op. cit., p. 29.

22. Cf. Thomas McPherson, 'The Argument from Design', p. 60; R. G. Swinburne, 'The Argument from Design' in 'Philosophy' (1968), and 'The Argument from Design — a Defence' in 'Religious Studies' (1972).

23. See R. W. Hepburn, 'Christianity and Paradox', chs. 3—4; also pp. 107—9 of the present book.

24. This is suggested by, for example, Smart's discussion in 'Philosophers and Religious Truth', ch. 5, 'Rudolf Otto and Religious Experience': Smart considers that mystical experience also can be accommodated in a theistic system.

25. 'Doctrine and Argument in Indian Philosophy', p. 144. The entire chapter is an interesting study of the relation between experience and interpretation in the Indian systems.

26. 'God who Acts', p. 23.
27. See ch. 8, p. 148 ff.
28. See chs. 4—5.

CHAPTER 3

1. 'Induction and Hypothesis' in 'Proceedings of the Aristotelian Society', Supplementary Volume (1937).

2. 'God and Philosophy', p. 141. My colleague Jonathan Barnes points out that almost any syllogism affords a counter-example to Flew's argument: 'If I have two leaky buckets and put one inside the other, I shall be able to carry water provided only that their holes do not coincide.'

3. As John Hick is inclined to do, cf. 'Arguments for the Existence of God', p. 110 f.

4. Cf. Basil Mitchell, 'The Grace of God' in 'Faith and Logic', ed. Basil Mitchell.

5. Richard Swinburne has an excellent account of the way in which different types of evidence may reinforce each other in 'The Concept of Miracle', ch. 6.

6. The problem thus presented is considered in Ch. 5, pp. 94—5.

7. 'Gods' in 'Proceedings of the Aristotelian Society' (1944—5); reprinted in John Wisdom, 'Philosophy and Psycho-Analysis'.

8. An example familiar to philosophers is the Sun—Line—Cave sequence in Books VI—VII of Plato's 'Republic'.

9. Reprinted in 'Andrew Marvell', ed. John Carey, pp. 179—210.

10. Cf. Helen Gardner, 'The Business of Criticism', p. 52: 'If it is a passage which we are interpreting, the final test is always the consistency of the interpretation of the passage with the interpretation of the work as a whole. If we are attempting the interpretation of a single complete work, the test is the reverse of this: does our interpretation of the whole make sense of the parts'.

11. 'Grammar of Assent', p. 230.

12. In 'Historia' (1958).

13. 'The Objectivity of History' in 'Philosophical Analysis and History', ed. W. H. Dray, pp. 86—7.

14. Ibid., p. 87.

15. The argument in fact assumes the form of a spiral and the pattern of such a spiral argument has been usefully analysed by Humphrey Palmer, in relation to source criticism as practised by biblical scholars:

A source-hypothesis is built up stage by stage, each successive version giving a new vantage point from which to survey the text and to pick out details newly thrown into prominence, to build the next stage with. To the constructor, each new detail seems to confirm his theory, and he goes on till all the details are used up. Then he publishes: that is, he describes how all those details look in the light of the theory. Brother critics learn the theory by description, not by constructing it. The details, which one by one he found to fit, are all received by them as part of the description of the theory. For them, such details cannot 'confirm': for to take part of a description as the confirmation of that description is, precisely, to argue in a circle.

This difficulty could be overcome by presenting the theory in the order of construction, critic and reader going through the text together perhaps half a dozen times. The reader would then see the theory growing as it feeds upon the text, and its logical shape would be seen to be spiral, not circular.

Palmer admits that several such spirals could be made and considers the objection that success in constructing a single such spiral does not show the theory to be true. He replies:

The critic did not frame his theory at each stage to fit the details he will discover in the next, but to suit those he did discover in the last. If those of the next stage fit the same theory, this cannot be just coincidence. Spiral argument is the critic's form of an experiment. The results are difficult to assess, because critics do not say what they would count as *dis*-confirming their theory. ('The Logic of Gospel Criticism', p. 165 ff.)

161

16. Op. cit., p. 156.
17. Ibid., p. 157.
18. Ibid., p. 159.
19. There are complications about the interpretation of a poem which do not, however, affect the main contention. Critics may differ (as, indeed, Brooks and Bush seem to do) as to whether the critic's task is to discover what the poet meant in writing as he did or what the poem, taken by itself, means; and this affects the relevance of biographical and other historical evidence. If may be argued that there is no single definitive answer to the question, 'What does the poem mean?', and that, therefore, there is no room here for truth or falsehood. But sometimes the sense of a poem is clear and unambiguous, and, even when it is not, there are some interpretations that can confidently be dismissed as false.

CHAPTER 4

1. Reprinted in 'New Essays in Philosophical Theology', ed. Flew and MacIntyre, p. 112.

2. A metaphysical system, in this sense, resembles an 'ideology' as described by Alasdair MacIntyre in 'The End of Ideology and the End of the End of Ideology' (reprinted in 'Against the Self-Images of the Age'). MacIntyre says of an ideology that it

attempts to delineate certain general characteristics of nature or society or both, characteristics which do not belong only to particular features of the changing world which can be investigated only by empirical inquiry. So for Christianity the God-created and God-maintained character of the world is just such a characteristic; so for Marxism the laws of dialectical change are such a characteristic. Two closely related queries can always be raised about this feature of an ideology: what is the status of statements about these general characteristics and how do we show such statements to be true or false? And what is the relationship between the truth or falsity of such

162

statements and the truth and falsity of scientific or historical claims about the character of empirically investigable processes and events? How for Christianity are claims about divine providence related to claims about historical events in first-century Palestine? How for Marxism are claims about the dialectic related to claims about the wage levels of the working class under industrial capitalism? (pp. 5—6).

MacIntyre notes as further features of an ideology that it has ethical implications and defines a social group. The importance of these features of Christianity will become apparent in Part III.

3. Op. cit., pp. 112—13.
4. This problem is discussed at the end of ch. 5, pp. 94-5.
5. 'Theology and Falsification' in 'New Essays in Philosophical Theology', p. 113.
6. R. W. Hepburn, 'Christianity and Paradox', p. 176.
7. 'God and Philosophy', p. 98.
8. T. S. Kuhn, 'The Structure of Scientific Revolutions'; see especially ch. 10.
9. Op. cit., pp. 117—18.
10. Ibid., pp. 110—11.
11. Ibid., p. 120.
12. Ibid., p. 121.
13. Ibid., pp. 121--2.
14. 'English Philosophy since 1900', p. 144.
15. 'The Structure of Scientific Revolutions', pp. 145—6.
16. Ibid., pp. 146—7.
17. Ibid., p. 148.
18. Ibid., p. 149.
19. 'Contemporary British Philosophy', 3rd series, ed. H. D. Lewis, p. 467.
20. Op. cit., p. 471.
21. 'Philosophy and Language', reprinted in 'The Concept of a Person and other Essays', p. 27.
22. Op. cit., p. 27.
23. Ibid., p. 21.
24. Ibid., p. 21.
25. Ibid., p. 21.

CHAPTER 5

1. See D. Z. Phillips, 'The Concept of Prayer'; also 'Death and Immortality'.

2. See R. G. Collingwood, 'Essay on Metaphysics', ch. 5.

3. See R. M. Hare's contribution to 'Theology and Falsification' in 'New Essays in Philosophical Theology'.

4. See R. B. Braithwaite, 'An Empiricist's View of the Nature of Religious Belief', reprinted in 'The Philosophy of Religion', ed. Basil Mitchell.

5. See John Hick, 'Meaning and Truth in Theology' in 'Religious Experience and Truth', ed. Hook, pp. 208—9.

6. See H. Richard Niebuhr, 'The Meaning of Revelation', p. 37 ff.

7. 'The Structure of Scientific Revolutions', p. 93.

8. 'Criticisms and the Growth of Knowledge', ed. Musgrave and Lakatos, p. 129.

9. Quoted from an earlier version of Lakatos's paper in 'Proceedings of the Aristotelian Society' (1968—9), p. 156.

10. Ibid.

11. 'Differences between Scientific and Religious Assertions' in 'Science and Religion; New Perspectives on the Dialogue', ed. I. G. Barbour.

12. For a fuller discussion of this point and of the whole question see C. R. Kordig, 'The Theory-ladenness of Observation' in 'Review of Metaphysics' (1971).

13. T. S. Kuhn, op. cit., p. 93.

14. Musgrave and Lakatos, op. cit., p. 239. The reference here is to Lakatos's distinction between 'progressive and degenerative problem-shifts', set out in his contribution to the symposium, p. 118:

Let us take a series of theories, T1, T2, T3, . . . , where each subsequent theory results from adding auxiliary clauses to (or from semantical re-interpretations of) the previous theory in order to accommodate some anomaly, each theory having at least as much content as the unrefuted content of its predecessor. Let us say that such a series of theories is theoretically progressive (or 'constitutes a theoretically progressive problem-shift') if each new

164

theory has some excess empirical content over its predecessor, that is, if it predicts some novel, hitherto unexpected fact. Let us say that a theoretically progressive series of theories is also empirically progressive (or 'constitutes an empirically progressive problem-shift') if some of this excess empirical content is also corroborated, that is, if each new theory leads us to the actual discovery of some *new fact*. Finally let us call a problem-shift *progressive* if it is both theoretically and empirically progressive, and *degenerating* if it is not.

15. Ibid., p. 239.
16. Ibid., p. 262.
17. Ibid., p. 261.
18. Ibid., p. 178.
19. Ibid., p. 232.
20. Ibid., p. 261.
21. 'Metaphysics', pp. 177—8.
22. Ibid., p. 182.
23. Ibid., p. 182.
24. 'Languages, Standpoints and Attitudes', pp. 59—60.
25. There is a trenchant criticism of the wrong sort of appeal to presuppositions in the field of biblical scholarship to be found in James Barr's 'Old and New in Interpretation', p. 176 ff. He argues that:

> Within Biblical scholarship proof and argument are carried out by operation with evidence and not by deduction from presuppositions . . . Neither will 'good' presuppositions guarantee the success of a study nor 'bad' ones in themselves invalidate it . . . The critic has also to produce a better organization of the evidential data under consideration . . .
>
> There may be *implied* criteria, but it is in the doing of the work with *this* evidence, however, and not in the form of presuppositions which could be formulated independently of this situation that the identification of the criteria may be made.

26. In Barbour (ed.), op. cit., p. 112.
27. Op. cit., p. 122.

CHAPTER 6

1. Terence Penelhum, 'Problems of Religious Knowledge', p. 133.
2. See p. 27.
3. 'God and Philosophy', p. 141.
4. Notably by Michael Polanyi in 'Personal Knowledge': see especially ch. 10.
5. Barbour (ed.), op. cit., pp. 115—6.
6. Ibid., p. 125.
7. R. Bultmann, 'Kerygma and Myth', p. 103.
8. Penelhum, op. cit., p. 129.
9. Ibid., p. 131.
10. Ibid., p. 110.
11. Ibid., p. 130.
12. J. Hick, 'Faith and Knowledge', p. 209.
13. 'Arguments for the Existence of God', p. 31.
14. R. W. Hepburn, 'Christianity and Paradox', pp. 55—6.
15. Hick, op. cit., p. 116.
16. Ibid., pp. 112—14.
17. Ibid., p. 110.
18. The sense of 'know' that I have in mind here and in the next chapter (pp. 119—20) is that in which a man cannot be said to know that p if there is some reason to thinking that p may turn out to be false. It would seem to be close to, if not identical with, A. R. White's amended version of Norman Malcolm's 'strong' sense of 'know', in which a man can be said to know that p only if no reasonable man could be expected to see how the claim that p could be invalidated. (See A. R. White, 'On Claiming to Know' in 'Philosophical Review' (1957), reprinted in 'Knowledge and Belief', ed. A. Phillips Griffiths.)
19. See ch. 8, p. 148 ff.
20. The parable appears in 'Gods' in 'Proceedings of the Aristotelian Society' (1944—5), reprinted in 'Philosophy and Psycho-Analysis'.

CHAPTER 7

1. See p. 125 of this chapter.
2. The argument of this section to the effect that political theories are implicit in the way men live in society and that these are influenced by fundamental conceptions of what it is to be a man is developed more fully by Isaiah Berlin in 'Does Political Theory still Exist?' in 'Philosophy, Politics and Society' (2nd series), ed. Laslett and Runciman. Cf:

> In so far as it is such fundamental conceptions of man that determine political doctrines (and who will deny that political problems, e.g. about what political groups can or should be or do, depend logically and directly on what man's nature is taken to be?), it is clear that those who are governed by these great integrating syntheses bring to their study something other than empirical data.
>
> If we examine the models, paradigms, conceptual structures that govern various outlooks whether consciously or not, and compare the various concepts and categories involved with respect, for example, to their internal consistency or their explanatory force, then what we are engaged upon is not psychology or sociology or logic but moral, or social or political theory, or all these at once . . . (op. cit., p. 28).

Later in the same essay (pp. 32–3) Berlin considers and rejects a familiar objection to this line of argument, viz. that all such theories are socially and economically conditioned.

3. The August Comte Memorial Lecture for 1964, reprinted in 'Metaphysics and Common Sense', p. 238.
4. Op. cit., p. 239.
5. This is what, e.g., Penelhum appears to have done in the passage quoted earlier (ch. 6, p. 99) where he says of an explanatory hypothesis in the sciences that in such a case 'some proposition is tentatively adopted, and our confidence in it is in proportion to the amount of confirmation it receives. If the evidence seems predominantly against it, it is abandoned' ('Problems of Religious Knowledge', p. 133).

6. 'The Impact of Science on Society', pp. 110—11, quoted in M. Polanyi, 'Knowing and Being', p. 94.

7. 'Knowing and Being', p. 94.

8. 'Philosophy and the Historical Understanding', ch. 8.

9. 'Reflections on the Revolution in France', p. 95.

10. For further discussion see my 'Neutrality and Commitment' (An Inaugural Lecture).

11. 'Belief', pp. 431—2.

12. Op. cit., p. 471.

13. The reference is to Plato's 'Republic', especially 'The Divided Line', Book VI, 509 D—511 E.

14. A consequence of the extent to which the system of belief as a whole transcends the scope and to some extent the understanding of the individual who accepts it is that the point of entry by different individuals into the system may vary widely. This is particularly evident in the non-scientific cases. For example a Marxist regards the law courts in capitalistic countries as devices for maintaining the power and promoting the interests of the bourgeoisie. Talk of the value of free institutions and the impartial administration of justice seems to him to be merely a misleading epiphenomenon. If he were to be converted to the liberal system, this would involve eventually a very large-scale restructuring of his system of beliefs. It might occur by way of a sudden conversion through witnessing a dramatic trial, or it might be a much more gradual affair. It might, indeed, be due to his reading works on political theory and jurisprudence, though it would be rare for these to take effect without experience of the system's working. In whatever way it happens, the consequence is that the individual now adheres to a system of belief whose ramifications he has some inkling of, but does not fully understand. The fact that 'points of entry' differ provides one explanation of the extent to which any large-scale system of belief tends to be interpreted in different ways and to develop within it different traditions. Different elements are emphasised along the many which contribute to the justification of the entire system; their importance may be exaggerated and, in consequence, the balance of the whole may be disturbed.

168

CHAPTER 8

1. See note 12 to ch. 5.
2. 'Metaphysical Beliefs', ed. MacIntyre, p. 205.
3. In 'Religious Experience and Truth', ed. Hook, p. 122.
4. 'Theology and Falsification' in 'New Essays in Philosophical Theology', ed. Flew and MacIntyre, pp. 103-4.
5. 'Kerygma and Myth', pp. 210-11.
6. 'The Nature and Destiny of Man', p. 165.
7. Karl Barth, *Church Dogmatics*, I/1, p. 350.
8. In 'Religious Experience and Truth', ed. Hook, p. 53.
9. 'Revelation' in 'Faith and Logic', p. 101.
10. 'Nature, Man and God', p. 315 f.
11. 'The Idea of Revelation in Recent Thought', p. 65 f.
12. 'The Church's use of the Bible', ed. D. E. Nineham, p. 165.

Select Bibliography

PART I

A. J. Ayer, 'Language, Truth and Logic' (Gollancz, 1946).
———, 'Philosophy and Language' in 'The Concept of a Person and other Essays' (Macmillan, 1963).
Jonathan Barnes, 'The Ontological Argument' (Macmillan, 1972).
Austin Farrer, 'Love Almighty and Ills Unlimited (Fontana, 1961).
J. N. Findlay, 'Can God's Existence be Disproved?' in 'New Essays in Philosophical Theology', ed. Flew and MacIntyre (S.C.M. Press, 1955).
Antony Flew, 'Divine Omnipotence and Human Freedom' in 'New Essays in Philosophical Theology', ed. Flew and MacIntyre.
———, 'God and Philosophy' (Hutchinson, 1966).
———, 'Theology and Falsification' in 'New Essays in Philosophical Theology'. See also replies by R. M. Hare, Basil Mitchell and I. M. Crombie in same volume.
Stuart Hampshire, 'Identification and Existence' in 'Contemporary British Philosophy', 3rd series, ed. H. D. Lewis (Allen & Unwin, 1956).
R. W. Hepburn, 'Christianity and Paradox (Watts, 1958).
John Hick, 'Arguments for the Existence of God' (Macmillan, 1970).
———, 'Evil and the God of Love' (Macmillan, 1966).
———, 'Faith and Knowledge' (Cornell U.P. 1957; 2nd ed. Cornell U.P. and Macmillan, 1966).
John Hick and A McGill (eds.), 'The Many-Faced Argument' (Collier-Macmillan and Macmillan, 1968).
Anthony Kenny, 'Necessary Being' in 'Sophia', vol. I (1962), no. 3.
———, 'The Five Ways' (Routledge & Kegan Paul, 1969).

J. L. Mackie, 'Evil and Omnipotence' in 'Mind', vol. 64 (1955). Reprinted in 'The Philosophy of Religion', ed. Basil Mitchell (O.U.P., 1971).

Norman Malcolm, 'Anselm's Ontological Arguments' in 'Philosophical Review', vol. 69 (1960). Reprinted in 'The Many-Faced Argument'.

C. B. Martin, 'Religious Belief' (Cornell U.P., 1959).

E. L. Mascall, 'Existence and Analogy. (Longmans, 1949).

———, 'He Who Is, a study in Traditional Theism' (Longmans, 1943).

G. B. Matthews, 'Theology and Natural Theology' in 'Journal of Philosophy', vol. 61 (1964).

Thomas McPherson, 'The Argument from Design' (Macmillan, 1970).

Kai Nielsen, 'Contemporary Critiques of Religion' (Macmillan, 1971).

Terence Penclhum, 'Divine Necessity' in 'Mind', vol. 69 (1960). Reprinted in 'The Philosophy of Religion', ed. Basil Mitchell.

———, 'Religion and Rationality' (Random House, 1971).

D. Z. Phillips, 'Death and Immortality' (Macmillan, 1970).

Alvin Plantinga, 'God and Other Minds: A Study of the Rational Justification of Belief in God' (Cornell U.P., 1967).

———, 'The Free Will Defence' in 'Philosophy in America', ed. Max Black (Allen & Unwin, 1965). Reprinted in 'The Philosophy of Religion', ed. Basil Mitchell.

I. T. Ramsey, 'Religious Language: An Empirical Placing of Theological Phrases' (S.C.M. Press, 1957).

Jerome Schaffer, 'Existence, Predication and the Ontological Argument' in 'Mind', vol. 71 (1962). Reprinted in 'The Many-Faced Argument'.

Ninian Smart, 'Doctrine and Argument in Indian Philosophy' (Allen & Unwin, 1964).

———, 'Philosophers and Religious Truth' (2nd ed., S.C.M. Press, 1969).

W. T. Stace, 'Mysticism and Philosophy' (Lippincott, 1960).

R. G. Swinburne, 'The Concept of Miracle' (Macmillan, 1970).

——, 'The Argument from Design' in 'Philosophy', vol. 43 (1968).

——, 'The Argument from Design — a Defence' in 'Religious Studies', vol. 8 (1972).

G. E. Wright, 'God who Acts' (S.C.M. Press, 1952).

PART II

J. Barr, 'Old and New in Interpretation' (S.C.M. Press, 1966).

Jonathan Bennett, 'Rationality' (Routledge & Kegan Paul, 1964).

R. B. Braithwaite, 'An Empiricist's View of the Nature of Religious Belief', Eddington Memorial Lecture, November 1955 (C.U.P., 1956). Reprinted in 'The Philosophy of Religion', ed. Basil Mitchell.

——, 'Scientific Explanation' (C.U.P., 1946).

Cleanth Brooks, 'Marvell's Horatian Ode' in 'English Institute Essays' (1947). Reprinted in 'Andrew Marvell', ed. John Carey (Penguin, 1969).

Douglas Bush, 'Marvell's Horatian Ode' in 'Sewanee Review', vol. 60 (1952). Reprinted in 'Andrew Marvell', ed. John Carey.

R. G. Collingwood, 'Essay on Metaphysics' (O.U.P., 1940).

——, 'The Idea of History' (O.U.P., 1946).

I. M. Crombie, 'Theology and Falsification' in 'New Essays in Philosophical Theology'.

P. J. Cuff, 'The Terminal Date of Caesar's Gallic Command' in 'Historia', vol. 7 (1958).

A. C. Danto, 'Analytical Philosophy of History' (C.U.P., 1965).

W. H. Dray, 'Laws and Explanation in History' (O.U.P., 1957).

D. M. Emmet, 'The Nature of Metaphysical Thinking' (Macmillan, 1945).

D. D. Evans, 'Differences between Scientific and Religious Assertions' in 'Science and Religion; New Perspectives on the Dialogue', ed. I. G. Barbour (S.C.M. Press, 1968).

Helen Gardner, 'The Business of Criticism' (Oxford, 1959).

A. Grünbaum, 'The Falsifiability of Theories: Total or Partial?' in 'Boston Studies in the Philosophy of Science 1961–2', ed. M. Wartofsky (Reidel, 1963).

R. M. Hare, 'Theology and Falsification' in 'New Essays in Philosophical Theology'.

C. G. Hempel, 'Aspects of Scientific Explanation' (Free Press, 1966).

R. W. Hepburn, 'Christianity and Paradox' (Watts, 1958).

H. A. Hodges, 'Languages, Standpoints, and Attitudes' (Clarendon Press, 1953).

John Hick, 'Meaning and Truth in Theology' in 'Religious Experience and Truth', ed. Hook (New York U.P., 1961).

C. R. Kordig, 'The Theory-ladenness of Observation' in 'Review of Metaphysics', (vol. 24, 1971).

T. S. Kuhn, 'The Structure of Scientific Revolutions' (Chicago U.P., 1962).

I. Lakatos and A. Musgrave (eds.), 'Criticism and the Growth of Knowledge' (C.U.P., 1965).

Basil Mitchell, 'The Grace of God' in 'Faith and Logic', ed. Basil Mitchell (Allen & Unwin, 1957).

———, 'The Justification of Religious Belief' in 'Philosophical Quarterly' (1961).

Alasdair MacIntyre, 'The End of Ideology and the End of the End of Ideology', reprinted in 'Against the Self-Images of the Age' (Duckworth, 1971).

E. Nagel, 'The Structure of Science' (Routledge & Kegan Paul, 1961).

R. Newell, 'The Concept of Philosophy' (Methuen, 1967).

J. H. Newman, 'The Grammar of Assent'.

H. Richard Niebuhr, 'The Meaning of Revelation' (Macmillan, 1960).

Humphrey Palmer, 'The Logic of Gospel Criticism' (Macmillan, 1968)

J. A. Passmore, 'Philosophical Reasoning' (Duckworth, 1961).

———, 'The Objectivity of History' in 'Philosophical Analysis and History', ed. W. H. Dray (Harper, 1968).

D. Z. Phillips, 'The Concept of Prayer' (Routledge & Kegan Paul, 1965).

Plato, 'Republic'.

Gilbert Ryle, 'Induction and Hypothesis' in 'Proceedings of the Aristotelian Society', Supplementary vol. 16 (1937).

D. Shapere, 'Meaning and Scientific Change' in 'Mind and Cosmos', ed. R. G. Colodny (University of Pittsburgh Press, 1966).

———, 'The Structure of Scientific Revolutions' in 'Philosophical Review', vol. 75 (1964).

F. Sibley, 'Aesthetic Concepts' in 'Philosophical Review', vol. 68 (1959).

C. Stevenson, 'Interpretation and Evaluation in Aesthetics' in 'Philosophical Analysis', ed. Max Black (Cornell U.P., 1950).

F. Waismann, 'How I see Philosophy' in 'Contemporary British Philosophy', 3rd series, ed. H. D. Lewis.

W. H. Walsh, 'Metaphysics' (Harcourt, Brace & World, 1955).

G. J. Warnock, 'English Philosophy since 1900' (O.U.P., 1958).

John Wisdom, 'Philosophy and Psycho-Analysis' (Blackwells, 1953).

———, 'Paradox and Discovery' (Blackwells, 1965).

PART III

Raziel Abelson, 'The Logic of Faith and Belief', in 'Religious Experience and Truth', ed. S. Hook (New York U.P., 1961).

J. L. Austin, 'Other Minds' in 'Proceedings of the Aristotelian Society', Supplementary Vol. 20 (1946). Reprinted in 'Philosophical Papers' (Clarendon Press, 1961).

A. J. Ayer, 'Man as a Subject for Science' (1964). August Comte Memorial Lecture, reprinted in 'Metaphysics and Common Sense' (Macmillan, 1969).

———, 'The Problem of Knowledge' (Penguin, 1956).

Michael Ayers, 'The Refutation of Determinism' (Methuen, 1968).

Peter R. Baelz, 'Christian Theology and Metaphysics' (Epworth Press, 1968).

174

John Baillie, 'Our Knowledge of God' (O.U.P., 1963).
———, 'The Idea of Revelation in Recent Thought' (O.U.P., 1956).
R. Bambrough, 'Reason, Truth and God' (Methuen, 1969).
Karl Barth, 'Church Dogmatics', vol. 1, part 1, 'The Doctrine of the Word of God', tr. G. T. Thomson and others (Clark, 1936).
———, 'Evangelical Theology: An Introduction' (Weidenfeld and Nicolson, 1963).
———, 'The Word of God and the Word of Man', tr. Horton (Harper, 1957).
H. W. Bartsch (ed.), 'Kerygma and Myth', vol. I, tr. Fuller (S.P.C.K., 1953).
Isaiah Berlin, 'Does Political Theory still exist?' in 'Philosophy, Politics and Society', 2nd series, ed. Lasiett and Runciman (Blackwell, 1962).
Brand Blanshard, 'Symbolism' in 'Religious Experience and Truth', ed. S. Hook.
Martin Buber, 'I and Thou', tr. R. G. Smith (Clark, 1937).
Rudolf Bultmann, 'Jesus and the Word', tr. L. P. Smith and E. Huntress (Weidenfeld & Nicolson, 1935).
Edmund Burke, 'Reflections on the Revolution in France'.
R. M. Chisholm, 'Theory of Knowledge' (Prentice-Hall, 1966).
A. C. Danto, 'Analytical Philosophy of Knowledge' (Cambridge, 1968).
Austin Farrer, 'Faith and Speculation' (Adam & Charles Black, 1967).
———, 'Free-Will and Determinism' (Black, 1958).
———, 'Revelation' in 'Faith and Logic', ed. Basil Mitchell (Allen & Unwin, 1957).
W. B. Gallie, 'Philosophy and the Historical Understanding' (Chatto & Windus, 1964).
Van A. Harvey, 'The Historian and the Believer' (S.C.M. Press, 1967).
William James, 'The Varieties of Religious Experience' (Macmillan, 1961).
H. D. Lewis, 'Our Experience of God' (Allen & Unwin, 1959).

Alasdair MacIntyre, 'The Logical Status of Religious Beliefs' in 'Metaphysical Beliefs', ed. MacIntyre (S.C.M. Press, 1957).

N. Malcolm, 'Knowledge and Belief' in 'Mind', vol. 51 (1952); reprinted in 'Knowledge and Belief', ed. A. Phillips Griffiths (O.U.P., 1967).

Basil Mitchell, 'Neutrality and Commitment', Inaugural Lecture (O.U.P., 1968).

Reinhold Niebuhr, 'The Nature and Destiny of Man' (Scribner, 1941; vol. 2, 1943).

Dennis Nineham (ed.), 'The Church's Use of the Bible', (S.P.C.K., 1963).

Rudolph L. Otto, 'Idea of the Holy', tr. J. W. Harvey (O.U.P., 1927).

David Pears (ed.), 'Freedom and the Will' (Macmillan, 1963).

T. Penelhum, 'Problems of Religious Knowledge' (Macmillan, 1971).

D. Z. Phillips, 'Faith and Philosophical Enquiry' (Blackwell, 1970).

—— (ed.), 'Religion and Understanding' (Blackwell, 1967).

Michael Polanyi, 'Knowing and Being' (Routledge & Kegan Paul, 1969).

——, 'Personal Knowledge' (Routledge & Kegan Paul, 1958).

H. H. Price, 'Belief' (Allen & Unwin, 1969).

Bertrand Russell, 'The Impact of Science on Society' (Allen & Unwin, 1952).

William Temple, 'Nature, Man and God' (Macmillan, 1933).

A. R. White, 'On Claiming to Know' in 'Philosophical Review', vol. 66 (1957). Reprinted in 'Knowledge and Belief', ed. A. Phillips Griffiths (O.U.P., 1967).

Index

Abelson, Raziel, 137
Action, 7-8
Activity, divine, 7, 32-3, 150-6
Analogy, problem of, 19-20
Anselm, St, 22
Apostasy, 140
Aristotle, 64-5, 131-2
Authority, chapter 7 *passim*
  in science, 123, 125
  in education, 128, 130
  of the Bible, 152-6
Ayer, A. J., 11, 14, 72-4, 119-20

Baillie, John, 149
Barnes, Jonathan, 159, 160
Barr, James, 165
Barth, Karl, 143-4, 146-7
Belief, degrees of articulateness in,
  132-3, 135
Berlin, Isaiah, 167
Berkeley, Bishop, 73
Bible,
  critical study of, 33, 148-56, 161,
  165
  inspiration of, 152-6
  authority of, 152-6
Blanshard, Brand, 144
'Bliks', 76, 93-4
Braithwaite, R. B., 76
Brooks, Cleanth, 47-51, 162
Buddhism, 145
Bultmann, Rudolf, 104, 141, 150
Burke, Edmund, 118, 125-6, 136
Bush, Douglas, 47-51, 162
Butler, Bishop, 148

Caesar, Julius, 52-3
Causality, 26-7
Churchill, Winston, 138
Collingwood, R. G., 76

Commitment,
  and rationality, chapter 7 *passim*
  in politics, 117-19, 125-8, 135
  in morality, 119-22
  unconditional, 104-5, 136-41
Conceptual schemes, 67, 74, 75, 91,
  115, 168
Conceptual differences, 62-3, 84, 90
Conversion, religious, 66, 70, 137
Cosmological argument, 24-7, 40-1
Criteria of assessment, 76, 80, 85, 88,
  95, 146
Crombie, I. M., 59-60, 63, 64
Cromwell, Oliver, 47-51
Culture clash, 82-3, 84
Cumulative case, 4, chapter 3 *passim*,
  111, 160
Cuff, P. J., 52-3

'Degenerative problem-shifts', 81, 136,
  164-5
Deism, 3
Determinism, 119-22
Duck-rabbit, 65

Education, 128-31
  commitment in, 129
  authoritarian, 128, 130
  liberal, 128, 130
Einstein, Albert, 70
Eliot, T. S., 147
'Eschatological verification', 11-15,
  110
'Essentially-contested concepts', 125
Evans, D. D., 79, 92-3, 94, 102
Evil, 9-10, 44-5
Exegesis, critical, 45-51, 60-2, 86-7, 90,
  155, 160, 161, 162
Explanation, 24-5, 26-7, 40-1, 67, 69,
  100

Explanatory hypothesis, 27, 99-105,
117, 121, 126
Explorers, parable of, 43-4, 60
Facts, in relation to theories, 77-80,
86-7
Faith,
in 'humanism', 123
in liberal democracy, 119
and knowledge, chapter 6 *passim*,
esp. 105-12
and reason, 137-8
and revelation, chapter 7 *passim*
religious and secular, chapter 7,
passim, 135, 139
as trust in God, 139
two senses of, 139, 141
Farrer, Austin, 28, 147
Findlay, J. N., 8-9
Flew, Antony, 26, 29, 30, 40, 64, 157,
159
Freedom of the will, 119-22
Freudianism, 62, 115

Galileo, 64-5
Gallie, W. B., 125
Gardener, parable of, 114-15
Gardner, Helen, 160
God,
and evil, 9-10
as active, 7-8, 32-3, 150-6
as 'experienced reality', 112-16, 121
as first cause, 26-7
as incorporeal, 7-8
as 'inferred entity', 112-16, 121
as necessary being, 8-9
as self-explanatory, 9, 25-6, 157
consistency of concept of, 7-10
logical coherence of concept of,
10-20
faith as trust in, 139
meaning of predicates applied to,
19-20
sense of presence of, 41, 107, 110,
112

Hampshire, S. N., 16-17
Hare, R. M., 76, 93-4
Hepburn, Ronald, 63, 64, 107-8, 159
Hick, John, 11-14, 22, 25, 29, 76, 105
105-12, 121, 158, 160
History, 33, 90
God's action in, 32-4, 150-6

objectivity of, 54-5
presuppositions of scientific, 33,
151
reasoning in, 51-3, 60-2, 89
and revelation, 33, 42, 111, 148-56
sacred and secular, 34, 150
Hodges, H. A., 88
'Humanism', 120-2, 137, 138-9, 150
Hypotheses,
explanatory, 100-5
scientific, 25, 123, 167

Identifying God, 16-18
Ideology, 162-3
Incarnation, doctrine of, 111, 150, 154
Incorporeality, problem of God's, 7-8
Inference, 112-16
Inspiration, divine, 62, 150-6
and infallibility, 155
Irrationalism, 84

James, William, 30
Jesus Christ, 11-12, 14, 110-11, 148
Jodrell Bank, 78
Johnson, Dr, 119, 120, 121
Judgement, historical, 55
role of personality in, 102-3, 125,
126
not rule-bound, 89
Justification by faith, 141-2

Kant, Immanuel, 22, 26
'Know', meaning of, 110, 112, 166
Knowledge and faith, chapter 6 *passim*,
esp. 105-12
Kordig, C. R., 164
Kuhn, T. S., 64-70, 73, 76-84, 90, 92,
122, 146

Lakatos, Imre, 77-82, 136
Liberal democracy, 117-19, 125, 127,
132, 137
Liberaliam, historical, 62
in educational theory, 128, 130
Lighthouse, sighting of, 112-13
Luther, Martin, 141

MacIntyre, Alasdair, 137, 162-3
Mackie, J. L., 157
McLean, M. R., 159
McPherson, T., 159
Malcolm, Norman, 21-4, 166
Marvell, Andrew, 47-51

178

Marxism, 62, 118, 137, 140-1, 168
Materialism, 85-6
Matthews, G. B., 157
Menuhin, Yehudi, 147
Metaphysics, 60-1, 71-4, 85-90, 130
Miracles, 33, 61
Mitchell, Basil, 160, 168
Mommsen, T., 52
Moral assessment, 88-9
    responsibility, 119-20

'Naive falsificationism', 77
'Naturalism', 120-2, 137, 138-9, 150
Necessary being, God as, 8-9, 21-4
Newman, J. H., 51
Niebuhr, H. R., 76
Niebuhr, Reinhold, 143, 146
Nielsen, Kai, 7, 11-15, 30, 31, 157
Nineham, Dennis, 154-5
Numinous, sense of, 15, 30-1

Observation, 78-9
Observation-languages, 68
Ontological argument, 21-3
    disproof of God's existence, 8-9
Order in the universe, 28-30
Otto, Rudolf, 30, 159

Palmer, Humphrey, 161
Paradigms, scientific, 64-70
    rational choice between, chapter 5
        passim
Passmore, J. A., 54-5
Paul, St, 141, 151
Penelhum, Terence, 105-12, 157, 159, 167
Perceptual analogy to faith, 108-9
Phenomenalism, 14
Phillips, D. Z., 76, 157
Philosophy, reasoning in, 71-4
Physicalism, 72-3
Pike, Nelson, 157
Plantinga, Alvin, 157
Plato, 132, 160
Polanyi, Michael, 123, 124, 127, 166
Popper, Karl, 54, 83, 84
Political theory and nature of man, 117
    117, 167
Politics and religion, analogies between,
    1, 2, 16, chapter 7 passim, 135,
    137
Politics, commitment, in, 117-9, 125-8,
    135

'Prejudice', 118, 125-6, 136
Probability, 29, 31, 39, 158
Presuppositions, 34, 75
    absolute, 76
    naturalistic, 149-50, 165
    rational choice between, 91, 93-4
Price, H. H., 130, 131
'Progressive problem-shifts', 81, 164-5
Proofs of God's existence, chapter 2
    passim
    ontological, 21-3
    cosmological, 24-7, 40-1
    teleological, 27-30, 40-1
'Radical theological non-naturalism',
    106
Radio optics, 78-9
Ramsey, I. T., 66
Rationality of theism, chapter 4 passim
    and culture, 135-6
Relativism, conceptual, 67, 106, 111
Religion and science, 91-5
Religious experience, 14-5, 30-2, 61,
    70   70, 86, 107-9, 115, 159
Resurrection, 152
Revelation, 32-4, chapter 8 passim
    and faith, chapter 7 passim
    and historical research, 33, 42, 111,
        148-56
    and reason, 142-8
    as communication, 145-6, 152-6
Ross, W. D., 121
Rules and rationality, 81, 84, 88-9
Russell, Bertrand, 124

Sanctity, 41
Scholars, disputes between, 45-6, 91
Science, authority in, 123
    commitment in, 123, 127
    development of, 122
    tradition in, 123
    and religion, 91-5
    as resting on faith, 93-4
Scientific hypotheses, 25, 123, 167
Scientific paradigms, 64-5, 65-6, 68, 69
    rational choice between, chapter 5
        passim
Scientific world view, 150-1
Self-explanatory, God as, 9, 25-6, 157
Self-involvement, 92, 103-4
Shaffer, Jerome, 23-4, 159
Smart, R. N., 15, 27, 28-9, 31, 159
Socrates, 132, 133

179

'Spiral arguments', 161
Stace, W. T., 15
Stranger, parable of the, 140
'Stratonician presumption', 26
Swinburne, R. G., 157, 159, 160

Teacher and pupils, analogy of, 153-5
Telekinesis, 8
Teleological argument, 27-30, 40-1
Temple, William, 148-9, 152
Tenacity, principle, of, 122
Theism, traditional Christian, 3,
    chapter 4 *passim*
Theology, biblical, 32-3
Tillich, Paul, 144
Tradition and culture, 126, 136
    and education, 129, 131, 136
    in science, 123

Verifiability, 11-16
'Verification, eschatological', 11-15,
    110
Verificationism, 68

Waismann, F., 71, 72
Warnock, G. J., 67, 71
Walsh, W. H., 85-7
White, A. R., 166
Wisdom, John, 45, 46, 114
Wittgenstein, L., 73
'Wittgensteinian fideism', 76
World-views, 60-1, 71-4, 85-90, 134,
    135

Zaehner, R. C., 15